A GUIDE TO

HOBSON'S CHOICE

SHELAGH HUBBARD

WITH TONY BUZAN

Hodder & Stoughton

Cover photograph ©: Brenda de Banzie and John Mills – The Ronald Grant Archive
Mind Maps: Ann Jones
Illustrations: Karen Donnelly

ISBN 0 340 75326 9

First published 1999
Impression number   10 9 8 7 6 5 4 3 2 1
Year   2002 2001 2000 1999

The 'Teach Yourself' name and logo are registered trade marks of
Hodder & Stoughton Ltd.

Typeset by Transet Limited, Coventry, England.
Printed in Great Britain for Hodder & Stoughton Educational, a division of
Hodder Headline Plc, 338 Euston Road, London NW1 3BH by Cox and Wyman Ltd,
Reading, Berks.

CONTENTS

There are five important things you must know about your brain and memory to revolutionize
the way you study:

◆ how your memory
  ('recall') works *while* you are learning
◆ how your memory works *after* you have finished learning
◆ how to use Mind Maps – a special technique for helping you
  with all aspects of your studies
◆ how to increase your reading speed
◆ how to prepare for tests and exams.

Recall during learning
– THE NEED FOR BREAKS

When you are studying, your memory
can concentrate, understand and
remember well for between 20 and 45
minutes at a time. Then it needs a break.
If you carry on for longer than this
without a break your memory starts to
break down. If you study for hours non-stop, you will remember
only a small fraction of what you have been trying to learn, and
you will have wasted hours of valuable time.

So, ideally, *study for less than an hour*, then take a five to ten
minute break. During the break listen to music, go for a walk, do
some exercise, or just daydream. (Daydreaming is a necessary
brain-power booster – geniuses do it regularly.) During the break
your brain will be sorting out what it has been learning, and you
will go back to your books with the new information safely
stored and organized in your memory banks. We recommend
breaks at regular intervals as you work through the Literature
Guides. Make sure you take them!

Recall after learning
– THE WAVES OF YOUR MEMORY

What do you think begins to happen to your memory straight after you have finished learning something? Does it immediately start forgetting? No! Your brain actually *increases* its power and carries on remembering. For a short time after your study session, your brain integrates the information, making a more complete picture of everything it has just learnt. Only then does the rapid decline in memory begin, and as much as 80 per cent of what you have learnt can be forgotten in a day.

However, if you catch the top of the wave of your memory, and briefly review (look back over) what you have been studying at the correct time, the memory is stamped in far more strongly, and stays at the crest of the wave for a much longer time. To maximize your brain's power to remember, take a few minutes and use a Mind Map to review what you have learnt at the end of a day. Then review it at the end of a week, again at the end of a month, and finally a week before your test or exam. That way you'll ride your memory wave all the way there – and beyond!

The Mind Map ®
– A PICTURE OF THE WAY YOU THINK

Do you like taking notes? More important, do you like having to go back over and learn them before tests or exams? Most students I know certainly do not! And how do you take your notes? Most people take notes on lined paper, using blue or black ink. The result, visually, is boring! And what does *your* brain do when it is bored? It turns off, tunes out, and goes to sleep! Add a dash of colour, rhythm, imagination, and the whole note-taking process becomes much more fun, uses more of your brain's abilities, and improves your recall and understanding.

A Mind Map mirrors the way your brain works. It can be used for note-taking from books or in class, for reviewing what you have just studied, and for essay planning for coursework and in tests or exams. It uses all your memory's natural techniques to build up your rapidly growing 'memory muscle'.

You will find Mind Maps throughout this book. Study them, add some colour, personalize them, and then have a go at drawing your own – you'll remember them far better! Stick them in your files and on your walls for a quick-and-easy review of the topic.

HOW TO DRAW A MIND MAP

1 Start in the middle of the page. This gives your brain the maximum room for its thoughts.
2 Always start by drawing a small picture or symbol. Why? Because a picture is worth a thousand words to your brain. And try to use at least three colours, as colour helps your memory even more.
3 Let your thoughts flow, and write or draw your ideas on coloured branching lines connected to your central image. These key symbols and words are the headings for your topic. Start like the Mind Map on page 7.
4 Then add facts and ideas by drawing more, smaller, branches on to the appropriate main branches, just like a tree.
5 Always print your word clearly on its line. Use only one word per line.
6 To link ideas and thoughts on different branches, use arrows, colours, underlining, and boxes (see page 24).

HOW TO READ A MIND MAP

1 Begin in the centre, the focus of your topic.
2 The words/images attached to the centre are like chapter headings; read them next.
3 Always read out from the centre, in every direction (even on the left-hand side, where you will have to read from right to left, instead of the usual left to right).

USING MIND MAPS

Mind Maps are a versatile tool – use them for taking notes in class or from books, for solving problems, for brainstorming with friends, and for reviewing and working for tests or exams – their uses are endless! You will find them invaluable for planning essays for coursework and exams. Number your main branches in the order in which you want to use them and off you go – the main headings for your essay are done and all your ideas are logically organized!

*S*uper speed reading

It seems incredible, but it's been proved – the
faster you read, the more you understand and
remember! So here are some tips to help you to practise reading
faster – you'll cover the ground more quickly, remember more,
and have more time left for both work and play.

◆ First read the whole text (whether it's a lengthy book or an
 exam or test paper) very quickly, to give your brain an
 overall idea of what's ahead and get it working. (It's like
 sending out a scout to look at the territory you have to
 cover – it's much easier when you know what to expect!)
 Then read the text again for more detailed information.
◆ Have the text a reasonable distance away from your eyes. In
 this way your eye/brain system will be able to see more at a
 glance, and will naturally begin to read faster.
◆ Take in groups of words at a time. Rather than reading
 'slowly and carefully' read faster, more enthusiastically.
◆ Take in phrases rather than single words while you read.
◆ Use a guide. Your eyes are designed to follow movement, so
 a thin pencil underneath the lines you are reading, moved
 smoothly along, will 'pull' your eyes to faster speeds.

*P*reparing for tests and exams

◆ Review your work systematically. Cram at the start of your
 course, not the end, and avoid 'exam panic'!
◆ Use Mind Maps throughout your course, and build a Master
 Mind Map for each subject – a giant Mind Map that
 summarizes everything you know about the subject.
◆ Use memory techniques such as mnemonics (verses or
 systems for remembering things like dates and events).
◆ Get together with one or two friends to study, compare
 Mind Maps, and discuss topics.

AND FINALLY...

Have *fun* while you learn – it has been shown that students
who make their studies enjoyable understand and remember
everything better and get the highest grades. I wish you and
your brain every success! ⸂ —(Tony Buzan)

HOW TO USE THIS GUIDE

This guide assumes that you have already read *Hobson's Choice*, although you could read 'Background' and 'The story of *Hobson's Choice*' before that. It is best to use the guide alongside the play. You could read the 'Who's who?' and 'Themes' sections without referring to the play, but you will get more out of these sections if you do refer to it to check the points made in these sections, and especially when thinking about the questions designed to test your recall and help you to think about the play.

The 'Commentary' section can be used in a number of ways. One way is to read a section of the play, and then read the Commentary for that section. Keep on until you come to a test section, test yourself – then have a break! Alternatively, read a section of the Commentary, then read that section in the play, then go back to the Commentary. Find out what works best for you.

'Topics for discussion and brainstorming' gives topics that could well feature in exams or provide the basis for coursework. It would be particularly useful for you to discuss them with friends, or brainstorm them using Mind Map techniques (see p. vi).

'How to get an "A" in English Literature' gives valuable advice on what to look for in a text, and what skills you need to develop in order to achieve your personal best.

'The exam essay' is a useful 'night before' reminder of how to tackle exam questions, and 'Model answer' gives an example of an A-grade essay and the Mind Map and plan used to write it.

The questions

Whenever you come across a question in the guide with a star ✪ in front of it, think about it for a moment. You could even jot down a few words in rough to focus your mind. There is not usually a 'right' answer to these questions: it is important for you to develop your own opinions if you want to get an 'A'. The 'Test yourself' sections are designed to take you about

10–20 minutes each – which will be time well spent. Take a short break after each one.

Page numbers

Page references are to the Heinemann (1992) edition. If you have another edition, the page numbers may be slightly different, although the acts will be the same.

Key to icons

THEMES

A **theme** is an idea explored by an author. Whenever a theme is dealt with in the guide, the appropriate icon is used. This means you can find where a theme is mentioned just by flicking through the book. Go on – try it now!

Choice or
'Hobson Choice'
Work and
self-improvement

Love and
marriage
Alcohol and
self-destruction

Female
emancipation
Meanness and
generosity

Family life

 STYLE AND LANGUAGE

This heading and icon are used in the Commentary wherever there is a special section on the author's choice of words and **imagery**.

Harold Brighouse – a 'Lancashire lad'

Hobson's Choice is set in Salford, Manchester's next-door neighbour. You may get some idea of what the area is like today from the television soap *Coronation Street*. The **setting** is important to the play because it is real. It is an area Harold Brighouse knew well, because it is where his father grew up. Harold himself was born nearby in Eccles in 1882 and was educated at Manchester Grammar School. For a time, he worked as a director of a cotton mill in Manchester, when cotton was a major source of employment – significantly for women as well as men.

The Manchester School of playwrights

A wealthy drama enthusiast, Annie Elizabeth Horniman, massively influenced Brighouse's career. In 1908 she financed the Gaiety Theatre in Manchester and encouraged local writers to write plays reflecting real life in the local community, and using the dialect of the area. A Manchester group including Brighouse began to write about their concerns. Brighouse himself wrote over 80 plays between 1909 and 1954. By far the best known, though, is this tale of Salford life – *Hobson's Choice* – first performed in 1915.

The First World War and votes for women

Although *Hobson's Choice* is set in 1870, the concerns of the play are those of the time when it was written. Brighouse was in France in 1914 at the beginning of the First World War, and he saw at first hand the lack of 'choice' people had when conscripted to fight. (Read the explanation of the play's title on p. 25 and think about why this is important.)

One of the central themes in the play is the role of women in society (see pp. 27–9). Maggie's struggles to change her life still seem relevant nearly a century later! Yet she is also a product of the time the play was written, when women were fighting hard for equal rights. Before the First World War, British women could not vote, and married women had no legal rights to their own money or property. The suffragettes had fought hard for women's emancipation. Just before the First World War started, the Cat and Mouse Act was passed by Parliament to discourage suffragette disruption. ○ Do you know what suffragettes did to draw attention to their struggle, and how they were punished?

During the First World War, women took over many jobs traditionally done by men. They worked in factories and on public transport. Lancashire women already had a long history of working in the textile industry, so working-class women had money and a level of independence unusual at that time. ○ As you revise *Hobson's Choice*, find out as much as you can about Maggie as a woman who represents issues of the place and time when Brighouse wrote the play. Build a Mind Map to record what you discover.

Comedy of manners, and a tragic fall

We can see literary influences in this play as well as influences of history and geography. Many writers around the beginning of the twentieth century wrote about marriage, often using humour to underline a moral or message. Shaw, Ibsen and Chekhov are three playwrights who explored this theme. This kind of exploration of everyday life and behaviour, sometimes by means of humorous exaggeration, is known as **comedy of manners**. Coincidentally, this genre of drama arose alongside women's first steps towards emancipation during the late seventeeth century especially as they began to gain work as actresses in the theatre.

The play also has links with the literary tradition of tragic drama. Tragedy shows how a great man (the tragic hero) may cause his own downfall through a character fault and misguided behaviour. The downfall of Henry Hobson as he loses his daughters and his business because of his excessive drinking and his self-centred, tyrannical behaviour has parallels with Shakespearian tragic heroes such as King Lear and characters in Hardy's novels like Michael Henchard in *The Mayor of Casterbridge*.

THE STORY OF HOBSON'S CHOICE

Act 1 _Proposal_

Alice, Vickey and Maggie are at work in their father's shoe shop whilst Henry Hobson sleeps off a hangover. Albert Prosser comes, intending to woo Alice. Instead, Maggie sells him new boots. Alice accuses Maggie of jealousy. Hobson complains about his daughters' attitude and clothes. He says he will marry them off if they do not obey him.

Mrs Hepworth praises Will Mossop for making the best pair of boots she ever had. Hobson is annoyed that Will may want more pay. Jim Heeler arrives to go with Hobson to The Moonraker's Arms. Hobson asks Heeler's advice about finding husbands for Vickey and Alice, though not for Maggie. Heeler explains that a bride needs a dowry and Hobson changes his mind.

Maggie acts upon Mrs Hepworth's praise of Will, and her father's suggestion that she is an 'old maid'. She tells Will that she has noticed his talents and proposes marriage to him. Will is astonished. He tells her he is engaged to Ada Figgins, however Maggie quickly gets rid of her.

Hobson is furious when Maggie reveals their marriage plans. When Hobson begins to beat Will, he surprises everyone, himself included. Will stands up to his boss, takes Maggie in his arms and kisses her. She is delighted; her father is amazed.

Act 2 _Wedding_

A month later, Alice and Vickey are running the shop, and things look bad. Hobson is in The Moonraker's and Maggie and Will's rival business is taking away Hobson's trade. Maggie and Will invite the sisters to their wedding. Alice and Vickey react snobbishly to the way Maggie has gone about things. She is marrying quietly, dressed in her 'Sunday best' outfit. She buys a brass shoe-ring for a few pennies. She has bought second-hand furniture for her basement home.

Maggie has a plan to help her sisters. Vickey's young man, Fred Beenstock, has found Hobson asleep after falling, drunk, into the cellar of his father's Corn Merchant's business. Alice's admirer, is a lawyer. He draws up a writ accusing Hobson of trespass, damage and spying. Fred leaves this for Hobson to find when he awakes. Meanwhile, they all set off to the wedding.

Act 3 *Celebration*

The three young couples celebrate in Maggie and Will's new home. They eat wedding cake and drink a toast to the bride and groom and Will makes a speech. In the middle of the party, Hobson arrives, desperate for Maggie's help to stop the court action.

Maggie forces him to agree to a bargain: Beenstock's will not take him to court provided that he lets Alice marry Albert and Vickey marry Fred. He agrees, though he is furious about the £500 Albert charges to keep the case quiet, which will pay for the two weddings. He leaves, disowning all three daughters.

Will is reluctant for the others to leave, but Maggie encourages them to go. Will practises his writing while Maggie goes to get ready for bed. Will is very nervous about being alone with her, and makes up a bed on the sofa. Maggie returns in her nightclothes and leads Will to the bedroom.

Act 4 *Success*

A year later, things look even worse at Hobson's. His home is a muddle; Tubby Wadlow, is frying bacon over an open fire; his shop is doing no trade, and Hobson is sick. Jim Heeler listens to Hobson's symptoms. It is obvious that he is suffering from chronic alcoholism. Doctor MacFarlane prescribes treatment needed to save Hobson's life: he must give up drinking, and one of the daughters must return to care for him.

All three sisters have good reasons not to return: Vickey is pregnant, Alice has a lovely new home and Maggie has a business. Maggie says she will leave the decision to Will and her sisters mock her. However, when Will arrives, we see how much he has changed. He assesses the stock and says that he will be doing Hobson a favour. His ultimatum is that Hobson must give him the business and agree to call the shop Mossop's. He forces Hobson to give way by threatening to take Maggie home and leave him to his fate. Maggie looks on with pride as Hobson shrinks, defeated.

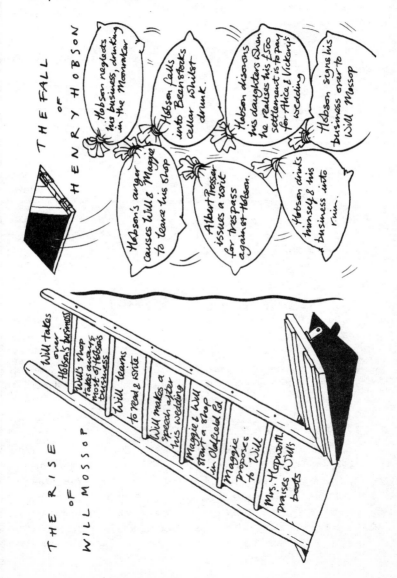

THE FALL OF HENRY HOBSON

- Hobson neglects his business, drinking in the Moonraker
- Hobson falls into Beanstork's cellar whilst drunk
- Hobson disowns his daughter's Joan he realises his £50 settlement is to pay for Alice & Vickey's wedding
- Hobson signs his business over to Will Mossop
- Hobson's anger causes Will & Maggie to leave his shop
- Albert Prosser issues a writ for trespass against Hobson
- Hobson drinks himself & his business into ruin

THE RISE OF WILL MOSSOP

- Will takes over Hobson's business
- Will's shop takes away most of Hobson's business
- Will learns to read & write
- Will makes a speech after his wedding
- Maggie & Will start a shop in Oldfield Rd
- Maggie proposes to Will
- Mrs. Hepworth praises Will's boots

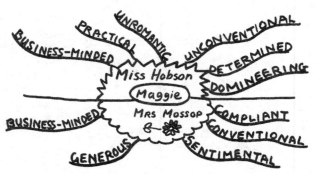

Miss Hobson

BUSINESS-MINDED · PRACTICAL · UNROMANTIC · UNCONVENTIONAL · DETERMINED · DOMINEERING

Maggie

Mrs Mossop

BUSINESS-MINDED · GENEROUS · SENTIMENTAL · CONVENTIONAL · COMPLIANT

Maggie

Before you begin to read about Maggie, look at the Mini Mind Map above. It sums up first impressions most people form of Maggie at the beginning of Act 1.

- ✪ Can you think of something she says, or does, in pages 1–17 as evidence for each characteristic?
- ✪ As the play moves on, what evidence reinforces your first impression?
- ✪ Which evidence makes you change your opinion about her character?
- ✪ When Miss Maggie Hobson becomes Mrs Maggie Mossop, does she change? Or do we just discover hidden aspects of her character?

THIRTY, ... AND SHELVED?

It is easy to see why Maggie is in charge in this family! Her mother has died. Her father spends most of his time in *The Moonraker's Arms*. Her sisters are more concerned with the latest fashions and eligible young men than the family business. Albert Prosser's visit shows a great deal about Maggie. This clever, hard-headed businesswoman sells him a pair of expensive boots before he has even had time to talk to

Alice. She is practical and unromantic in her attitude to courting comparing it to a *slipper with a fancy buckle ... all glitter and no use to nobody.* ✪ Is she envious of her prettier younger sisters? When her father decides it is best to get them off his hands by finding them husbands, she asks, '*Don't I get one?*' He laughs, saying she is *past the marrying age.* She soon proves him wrong. After Mrs Hepworth praises Will, Maggie proposes marriage to him. But what sort of marriage is she proposing?

A WORKING PARTNERSHIP

✪ Is Maggie planning a business partnership with Will? She says that two things keep Hobson's shop going: *the good boots you make* and *the bad boots other people make and I sell.* She shows good sense when she sends away Ada Figgins because she is not strong enough to help Will's prospects. But there is another, softer, Maggie, who admits, '*I've watched you for a long time, and everything I've seen I've liked.*' When Will tells her *without there's love between us* marriage would not come to much, she immediately replies, '*I've got the love all right.*'

She manipulates her father to take a belt to her future husband. When Will responds by kissing her and tells Hobson that the two of them will leave and set up in business themselves, her delight is clear.

✪ Do you think it is acceptable for a woman to ask a man out, or propose marriage? Why?
✪ What do you think about Maggie's view that romantic courtship is unnecessary before marriage? Include your views as you expand your Mind Map.
✪ What chance of happiness in marriage do you think Maggie and Will have? List as many points as you can for and against a happy future.

IT'S NEWS TO ME WE'RE SNOBS IN SALFORD

Maggie repeatedly defies convention. She rebels against her father when she decides to marry, and her choice is an uneducated man from a poor background. She sets up home in a cellar dwelling, the poorest sort of housing. She buys her furniture second hand. Her wedding is unromantic: no special clothes or expensive celebrations for Maggie. Her wedding ring is a brass shoe-ring, cost fourpence, from her father's shop.

● Do you agree with Maggie that a smartly furnished home and fancy wedding ceremony are not essential starts to married life? Or do you think waiting until you can afford to pay for these things might be a benefit to an engaged couple?

AN EMANCIPATED WOMAN

Maggie represents 'the modern woman'. She rejects the convention that woman are inferior, submissive partners of men. First impressions make her seem both domineering and dominant over every man she knows. She refuses to obey her father and marries without his approval. She bulldozes Will into marriage, a business and an education as relentlessly as she bulldozes Albert into walking through the streets of Salford pushing a hand-cart. She even drags her husband to bed *by the ear* on their wedding night, which is hardly the conventional way you would expect a 'blushing bride' to behave!

● How do you react to Will's comment about his new shop: *I dunno so much about being master?* Revise what you have learnt in Acts 2 and 3. What evidence can you find that Maggie will be the bossy wife of a hen-pecked husband? What evidence is there that their relationship gradually becomes more equal?

THE SOFTENING OF MAGGIE MOSSOP

You will need to decide for yourself whether Maggie changes over the year the play depicts, or whether Maggie Mossop in Act 4 is actually revealing qualities of character hinted at throughout the play. (● Or is it a bit of each?)

Maggie's marriage to Will certainly becomes a genuine love match. The romantic side of Maggie hinted at in Act 1 is reinforced when she keeps a flower from her wedding bouquet to press in her Bible, saying to Will, '*I'm not beyond liking to be reminded of this day.*' There is also a physical aspect to her affection: she surprises Will by holding his hands the first time the two are alone. At the end of Act 3 she startles him by putting her hands on his shoulders and we can only assume she startles him even more as she leads him to the bedroom!

Her pride in Will shows as she talks to Doctor MacFarlane, her father and, later on, her sisters of *my husband*. The genuine closeness between them is evident at the end as they discuss the outcome of Will's negotiations about the business. They are equal partners in business as in marriage. Maggie's determination to keep the brass wedding ring, when Will offers to buy a gold one, is followed by one of the most touching moments in the play. They kiss, and the words they speak – *Eh, lad!* and *Eh, lass!* – are loaded with real love and affection.

What can you remember?

?   Look back to the questions at the beginning of the section. Make notes in answer to them. Think of a quotation or other evidence for each point. The Mind Map on p. 6 will help you with this task.

Will Mossop

Will Mossop develops as a character even more than Maggie. The role is a challenge for any actor: if the transformation is to seem believable, the changes must not entirely contradict the man he is in Act 1.

Questions to consider about Will:
- ❂ Where is his potential to become a successful man hinted at during his early appearances on stage?
- ❂ How much of his success is a result of Maggie's influence on him?
- ❂ How does the name 'Will' reflect his prospects?

On pp. 47 and 51 of the Commentary, there are suggestions to help you make a Mind Map of the development in Will's character.

THE RAW MATERIAL OF A CHARMING MAN ...

Will's first appearance certainly gives him plenty of room to rise up in the world! He emerges only half-way out of Hobson's cellar, shy, awkward and poorly dressed. The stage direction says a *very keen eye* is needed to see his potential. Mrs Hepworth recognises his extraordinary talent as a bootmaker, but he has little else to recommend him. He is tongue-tied and hardly able to read. '*He's like a rabbit*' says Mrs Hepworth as he disappears back into the cellar.

There he might have stayed, but for Maggie. She describes him as *a natural born genius at making boots* which is inaccurate, for no one is naturally a genius at anything. Will has had the opportunity to learn boot-making at Hobson's and has become very talented. He is observant enough to have noticed Maggie's efficiency in the shop (and that she is *a shapely body*!). He is quick to see that they could become a successful *working partnership*. The talents and the charm are there: all it takes is someone to unlock Will's potential.

Will has had few opportunities to make anything of himself. He is the son of an illegitimate nobody: *a workhouse brat*. Ada Figgins indicates Will's social background: the poorest of the working class, uneducated and without the ambition to progress any further in the world. ○ How do these details remind you that Victorian society was different from the modern world?

MAGGIE'S INFLUENCE CHANGES WILL

Marriage to *the master's daughter* is, initially, a frightening prospect: as beyond Will's expectations as working in *the big shops in Manchester*. However, he soon begins to develop his potential. Plenty of evidence indicates that Maggie does not make Will into someone different: she just allows him to develop latent abilities. He grows in stature when faced with Hobson's anger about the proposed marriage and astonishes himself even more than Maggie when he threatens to leave and set up his own business.

A month later, he is both surprised and delighted by the novelty of having his own home and business, including business cards which announce his status as *William Mossop, Master Bootmaker*. He jokes that, though his name is on the windows, *'I dunno so much about being the master.'* However, Maggie provides him with ample opportunities to learn that role too.

Loyalty is Will's enduring characteristic: this, as well as fear of the unknown, bound him both to Hobson's and to Ada. That loyalty is rapidly transfered to Maggie. She changes Will's life beyond recognition and his gratitude grows into affection. When Maggie asks how he feels about making marriage vows, his sincerity shows in his answer: *'You're growing on me, lass. I'll toe the line with you.'* ○ Can you find evidence that Will's naivity causes the audience to feel affection for him, rather than judging him to be stupid, during the middle section of the play? Add your ideas about this to your Mind Map.

WILL'S EDUCATION

Maggie gives Will opportunities he never had from formal schooling and he proves to be a *very apt pupil*. In the month between the proposal and the wedding, Maggie teaches Will how to make a bridegroom's speech and to read and write. He is able to hold a conversation with Albert and Fred and with Hobson himself. He is developing a quick wit and a knowledge of a world outside Salford.

His relationship with Maggie is more difficult to pin down. He sometimes seems 'hen-pecked' as he carries furniture out of Hobson's and washes dishes, yet when she encourages him to act the part of master in his own house, he rises to the occasion. Everything Maggie does contributes to Will's education to be a confident partner in their marriage, including that memorable moment when she leads him to bed by the ear. ○ Will's progress is uneven. Can you think of three or four moments in Acts 2 and 3 when you admire him, and three or four moments when you feel sympathy or pity for him?

SUCCESS

The writing lesson at the end of Act 3 helps to prepare us for Will's progress in the year that follows. He finds his *room at the top* in a literal sense: when next seen by Vickey and Alice, he is up a ladder confidently estimating the value of Hobson's stock. Once again, Maggie puts him into the role of master and his performance is flawless. From the moment he appears, he exudes self-confidence and authority: '*Don't let us be too long about this,*' he says to Hobson, '*I'm busy at my shop.*' Will's education is complete: '*You're the man I've made you and I'm proud,*' says Maggie. He has the business sense to negotiate a good deal with Hobson, the ambition to see a future in St Ann's Square and the determination to get his own way, even prevailing over Maggie about the shop's name.

 Yet we must be able to believe this is the same Will. He retains a modesty about himself: '*I weren't by half so certain as I sounded,*' and a likeable ordinariness, which Hobson clearly prefers to his proud younger daughters. His gratitude and genuine affection show in his promise to replace Maggie's brass wedding ring with a gold one. He ends the play by echoing the expression of amazement with which he greated her proposal of marriage, but this time with the addition of a note of triumph for all they have achieved: '*Well, by gum!*'

Now try this

? Make a Mind Map to show the changes in Will as the play progresses (like the one for Maggie on p. 6).

Henry Horatio Hobson

Before you read about Henry Hobson, think about these questions.
- ✪ Why are we able to feel sympathy for this selfish bully?
- ✪ Why is he like a tragic hero (a man with many admirable qualities who brings about his own downfall by a weakness in his character)? (See the notes about a tragic fall on p. 5.)

A PARENT OF THE PERIOD

 Henry Hobson is a man of importance, in his own little world. His domination of his daughters is evident before he even appears on stage: he is their first topic of conversation and he intimidates them. They are waiting for him to go out, knowing he will have a bad temper after his night's drinking. Even Alice's young man, Albert, turns to leave when he hears Hobson is still there. Alice's defence of Albert's visits shows the extent of Hobson's control: *'father won't have us go courting.'*

Hobson's entrance confirms what the girls have already said. The stage direction describes him as *fifty-five, coarse, successful*. His status in the local community is reflected in the tall hat (working men wore flat caps) and his gold watch chain with its masonic emblems (see p. 44 to read about the Freemasons.) His complexion is *florid*. ✪ Does this hint at the weakness which causes his eventual downfall?

He is a bullying tyrant to his daughters. He straddles a chair aggressively and lectures them about their *uppish* attitude towards him, their *immodest* dress and how they are damaging *the fair name ... of Hobson*. Several times during the play he talks about the loss of his wife. Though relieved to have escaped from her control, he misses her influence on his daughters and he is determined to keep the upper hand, which is ironic, as Maggie seems to have taken over her mother's role. She keeps him in order, reminding him firmly what time dinner will be ready.

His meanness is shown by the way he expects the girls to work in his shop as well as running the home, but pays them no wages. Likewise, his plans to find husbands for Alice and Vickey are quickly dismissed when Jim points out that it necessitates paying dowries.

THE BEST DEBATER IN THE MOONRAKER'S PARLOUR

At the root of much of Hobson's behaviour, and the cause of the downfall of both himself and his business, is the amount of time he spends drinking with his friends. He is a tactless, selfish man and alcohol makes matters worse by dulling his thinking. Every time he appears, he is either unpredictable and bad-tempered because he has a hangover, or illogical and aggressive because he has been drinking. In a hungover state, he threatens to choose husbands for his younger daughters but, cruelly, tells Maggie she is *past the marrying age*. He flies into a rage when he realizes his daughters have tricked him into giving them dowries and disowns the three of them. He is abusive to several people who, later, attempt to care for him, even arguing with the doctor and rejecting the treatment which will cure his alcoholism.

After drinking, he takes a strap to Will, an act that leads to Will and Maggie leaving the shop. Once they have gone, his business can no longer survive the neglect it suffers while Hobson is in The Moonraker's. More immediately, drink causes Hobson's actual fall into the Beenstock's cellar. ✪ How do the consequences of this fall speed up the decline both of Hobson and his business?

BRITISH MIDDLE CLASS AND PROUD OF IT

Hobson's pride in his status underlies much of what he says and does. The success of his business comes from honest hard work (though not his own in recent times) and the company he keeps is local shopkeepers like himself – big fish in the small sea of Chapel Street, Salford – Jim Heeler, a grocer, Tudsbury, a draper and Sam Minns, a publican. He despises lawyers because they have status and wealth but do not work in the sense he recognizes, but maintains respect for Will and Maggie as shopkeepers who talk his language. Hobson criticizes his younger daughters for imitating the fashions of the upper classes, yet, with his habitual lack of logic, he is comically obsequious to Mrs Hepworth, on his knees *fondling her foot* as soon as she walks through the door.

His need to protect his status in the community sends him to Maggie when he finds himself in trouble with the law after his fall. Will's naive comments about reports in the newspaper persuade Hobson that a settlement out of court is his only option. The fear of losing his respectable reputation even overcomes his meanness. ✪ What evidence can you find that Hobson is neither as worldly-wise nor as confident as he likes to appear, especially in Act 3 of the play?

HAVE YE NO FEMALE RELATIVE THAT CAN MANAGE YE?

Like most bullies, Hobson cannot deal with people who stand up to him and, at the end, three people stand their ground against his blustering bad temper. First, Doctor MacFarlane gains his respect, despite being *foreign*, and forces Hobson to admit to alcoholism.

Second, he is touchingly grateful when Maggie returns to look after him: '*I didn't want you when the doctor said it, but, by gum, I want you now.*'

Third, and most unexpected for Hobson, is when Will Mossop stands up to him. Hobson crumbles when he realizes that either Will gets his own way, or Maggie cannot come back. His initial offer, to give Will back his old job is laughable, however Will's decision that the only terms he will consider are to take over the business, with Hobson as a sleeping partner, and that the shop be renamed Mossop and Hobson, leaves Hobson *crushed-like*. He has lost control of the business that gave him his status.

It says a lot for Brighouse's ability to create a believable, rounded character, that Hobson ends with the sympathy of the audience, rather than the judgement that he got just what he deserved.

What can you remember?

? Record the two sides of Hobson on a Mind Map: his less-attractive characteristics and examples of incidents in the play when you dislike him, then his more likeable characteristics and incidents in the play when you feel sympathy for him.

Now you have met the three most important and believable characters, take a break before you think about the minor characters and their functions in the play.

Alice and Vickey Hobson

Maggie's younger sisters seem to be included mainly so their failings contrast with her good points.

⊘ Where can you find examples of contrast with Maggie?

⊘ Where does Maggie's behaviour towards her sisters emphasize her good qualities?

Hobson's two younger daughters are selfish, lazy and snobbish. His description of them dressed in their fashiononable bustles, *with a hump added to nature behind you ... The hump was wagging, and you put your feet on the pavement as if you had chilblains* sums up their conceit in a humorous way. Their snobbish rejection of Will Mossop continues throughout the play. They are unable to forget that he began work as their boothand. They are horrified when the couple set up in business in a cellar and continue to dismiss Will even when it is self-evident that he has got on in the world.

Alice is the middle sister, aged 23. She deputizes for Maggie in the shop, though not very well. We first see her knitting and carrying on her courtship with Albert when she ought to be working. When Maggie leaves she is unable to manage the accounts, Tubby or her father. She expresses the wish to be *married and out of it*. Albert is her choice because she sees marriage to a solicitor as a means of rising in society. By the end of the play she has achieved her goal, refusing to return to Chapel Street because she lives *in the Crescent*. The importance Alice attaches to appearance and material things is evident throughout: she is very critical of Maggie buying second-hand furniture and getting *married with a brass ring*.

Vickey, the youngest of the three at 21, is described as *pretty*. She is even less practical than Alice and spends her time in the shop, reading. She is more emotional than her older sisters: her affectionate greeting when Hobson is ill is a contrast with Alice's haughty attitude. Also, her reason for not returning to her father is a *child coming*, rather than status or possessions. She can be spiteful: she is the one who tells her father about Maggie and Will. It is her suspicion that Maggie and Will might exploit their closeness to Hobson to inherit his money if he should die. She makes some vicious comments, saying Will *hasn't the spirit of a louse* and making her final exit with the insult *beggars on horseback.*

These self-centred women have little sense of family loyalty: they lack gratitude to the sister who enabled them to marry, they fail to do their duty as daughters when their father is sick. Most telling, they both publicly criticize their husbands; Alice when she tells Albert to to sit down and be quiet, Vickey when she dismisses Maggie's need to consult Will about returning to her father. Their marital happiness is a big question-mark.

Think about it

? What characteristics does Alice share with Maggie, and how is she different?

? What qualities does Vickey share with Maggie (if any) and how is she different?

? What do you think of their choice of husbands? Whose marriage is likely to be happier, Vickey's or Alice's?

Albert Prosser and Fred Beenstock

Just as her sisters contrast with Maggie, their young men offer a contrast to Will. Both sons of affluent families, thus suitable husbands for young ladies who wish to better themselves through marriage. They also make Maggie's plan to gain dowries for her sisters possible: Fred provides the cellar and Albert provides the legal expertise to bribe Hobson.

Albert is junior partner in the family firm of solicitors, Prosser, Pilkington and Prosser. However, he might not have done so well if he had had to make his own way in the world. He is easily dominated, beginning the play being forced to buy an expensive pair of boots: a pound would have been a week's wages for a working man at that time. He is frightened of Hobson and calls at the shop only when he knows Alice's father is out. She dominates him, too, curtly stopping him from making a speech in reply to Will at the wedding. ✪ Why is her reason for this ironic, considering Albert's profession?

He is a good match for Alice, obsessed with appearance (Maggie notes his spending on *laundry bills and hair cream*) and expensive possessions. He is the one who notices Mrs Hepworth's costly hot-house flowers. His snobbishness is emphasized when Maggie makes him wheel the broken chairs across Salford on a hand-cart and Albert is appalled at the thought that his friends might see him. His greed shows when he demands a £1,000 settlement from Hobson.

Fred is less developed as a character. He is employed in his family's wholesale grocery business, Jonathan Beenstock and Co., Corn Merchants. He is described as *attractive though not at all a blood*. He is an affable young man, uncomplainingly doing as Maggie tells him: he runs to bring Albert, helps Will carry a sofa downstairs and does his share of the washing up. He is a good catch for Vickey, *in ... business, not trade*. One suspects that she will be the dominant partner in that marriage, though. As her father says of the two young husbands-to-be, *'they'll know what marrying a woman means before so long.'*

○ Do you think Maggie is correct that Will's success in business will ensure that he ends up the wealthiest of the three? Why? What does Will have that Albert and Fred have not?

Tubby Wadlow and Jim Heeler

These men are important in Hobson's life. Timothy (Tubby) Wadlow is his foreman bootmaker, a long-serving, loyal employee. Jim Heeler is Hobson's trusted friend and drinking companion.

Tubby's role is important, despite his low social status. He is Will's boss and taught him the trade of bootmaking. He kindly agrees to provide Will with a home when Will becomes engaged to Maggie. As Hobson's business declines, Tubby's loyalty is constant. After Maggie leaves, he knows the business better than his employers, but he recognizes that his place is to receive orders, not to give them. He even takes on the role of house-keeper when Hobson makes the foolish decision to run his business only with men. He is more than ready to bring Maggie back to Hobson. His loyalty to the family deserves ample reward once Will and Maggie return to the shop, and his fortunes to rise with theirs.

Jim is loyal to Hobson in a different capacity. He is Hobson's *boon companion* and the man Hobson turns to for advice. His opinions on fathering reflect Hobson's: he too has daughters, but he has the advantage of a wife to reinforce his discipline. She seems to have some control over Jim, so his descent from regular drinker to excessive *toper* is less advanced than Hobson's. Jim provides sound advice to Hobson when he tells him to marry off his daughters and reminds him that dowries will be expected. He is surprised that the girls are expected to work without pay.

He is quick to come to Hobson's aid when he is ill. In the end, though, he is unable to help as he can see no serious fault in Hobson. He flatters him, saying he speaks as well as John Bright, a Victorian politician and famous orator. He will hear no criticism of Hobson's *temper and obstinacy* and, foolishly, tries to persuade Hobson to ignore Dr MacFarlane. Jim Heeler is too like Hobson to prove a real friend though he certainly serves the purpose of highlighting many of Hobson's weaknesses.

❂ Of these two men, which one do you think has the most consistently sound judgement? Is Brighouse making a point about the effects of alcohol? Or the nature of true friendship? Or is he criticizing the way social class was sometimes taken to indicate a person's intelligence?

Mrs Hepworth and Ada Figgins

Mrs Hepworth and Ada each appear only once, and represent opposite ends of the Salford social spectrum. Mrs Hepworth is a wealthy lady who illustrates Will's future potential as clearly as Ada demonstrates his current limits.

Ada is an obstacle to Will when Maggie proposes marriage, for he is 'tokened' (engaged) to her. She is no competition for Maggie: she will be no help in bettering Will's life. Ada would fulfil the stereotyped role of a submissive wife, trusting her husband to plan the future. Ada would hold Will back as certainly as Maggie will push him forward. She is *not ridiculous* – that would affect our estimation of Will – but she is weak, poor, uneducated, and naive.

She indicates where Will's future lies if he marries her: *a slave and a contented slave*. She is too weak to fight Maggie for Will, backing down with the complaint that *it's daylight robbery*. She has served her purpose as a minor character by that proving that Maggie is the right person to marry Will.

Mrs Hepworth, in contrast, arrives in a carriage and lives at Hope Hall, but certainly is not a snob. She stands for customers who appreciate fine workmanship, good service and can afford to pay for the best. That she found Will's boots in Chapel Street rather than St Ann's Square does not affect her opinion, and she appreciates Maggie's professionalism as a saleswomen, by comparison with Hobson's combination of grovelling on the floor and evading her questions in case she makes a complaint.

Although stereotyped as the domineering lady on stage, her other qualities, such as her generosity and her shrewdness, have a lasting effect on the whole play. Her visit prompts Maggie's proposal; then she becomes their benefactress. Contact with Mrs Hepworth and her kind teaches Will a thing or two. By the end, he plans to make Hobson's more attractive to wealthy customers and is no longer intimidated by the idea of taking his business to an environment where *the carriage trade* might expect to find the best-made boots in Lancashire!

○ What qualities does Mrs Hepworth share with Maggie? What do you think Maggie would have learned from contact with people of this social class?

Doctor MacFarlane

Domineering Scottish Doctor MacFarlane also appears only once. His specific purpose is to stand up to Hobson and break down his obstinacy. The doctor is a stereotyped character, almost a caricature: a dour Scotsman who is as blunt as a Lancastrian. He is as stubborn as Hobson, refusing to diagnose Hobson's illness until Jim Heeler stops interfering, then refusing Hobson's payment when he rejects the treatment prescribed for his *chronic alcoholism*. One contrast between these men is that the doctor, though angry, never becomes abusive. His temper shows only in the strengthening of his Scottish accent. His stubbornness leads to his refusal to let Hobson poison himself. He leaves only after he has ensured that Maggie is the right woman to enforce the discipline Hobson needs to survive. ❂ What evidence can you find that, despite his abrasive manner, the doctor is generous and caring.

Test yourself

? Learn this mnemonic to help you remember the names of the nine minor characters:

All   Vicious   Albatrosses   Fly   To   Japan Adopting Heartless   Manners
Alice Vickey   Albert   Freddie Tubby   Jim   Ada   Hepworth MacFarlane

? Which of these is an important characteristic of each of the nine minor characters:
   loyal, vain, snobbish, generous, helpless, stubborn, affable, uncritical, spiteful.
   Note down evidence for each one.

? Who said each of these lines, and how does it reflect the character who said it?
   A *'Suppose poor father gets worse and they are here ...'*
   B *'The man's a treasure, and I expect you underpay him.'*
   C *'I grant you're regular, but you don't exceed.'*
   D *'Wait till I get you to home, my lad. I'll set my mother onto you.'*
   E *'All right, Maggie.'*
   F *'You're a dunderheaded lump of obstinacy, but I've taken a fancy to ye, and I decline to let ye kill yeself.'*
   G *'I'd sooner stay single than have other people's cast-off sticks in my house.'*

Answers: A Vickey; B Mrs Hepworth; C Jim Heeler; D Ada Figgins; E Fred Beenstock; F Doctor MacFarlane; G Alice.

Now take a well-earned break

Minor characters involved in development of themes

	💍 (ring)	⚥ (gender)	👥 (family)	🪜 (ladder)	🍾 (bottle)	👞 (shoe)	(mouth)
Alice/ Vickey	Marry for status and possessions – especially Alice.						Vickey's suspicions about Hobson's will.
Albert/ Freddie		Reluctantly wash dishes after Maggie and Will's wedding.		Both born into family business – privileged.			
Tubby				Loyal to Hobson and works hard for him.			
Jim			Wife responsible for discipline of daughters.				
Ada		A stereotyped helpless, submissive woman.					Lack of money and education – she has few choices in life.
Mrs Hepworth						Lends money to set up Will's shop.	
Doctor MacFarlane					Diagnoses Hobson's illness and prescribes treatment.		

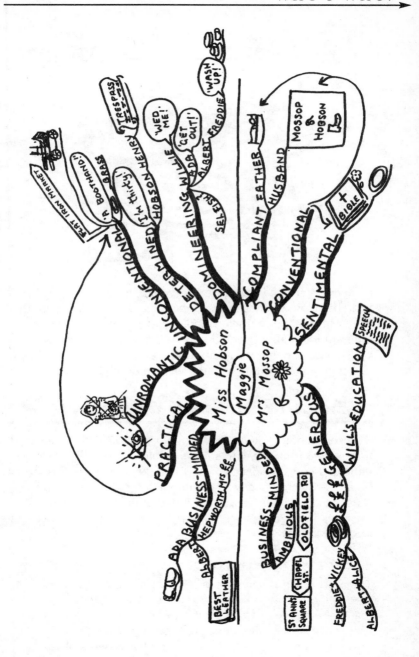

23

THEMES

A **theme** is an idea or issue explored by an author throughout a text. The main themes of *Hobson's Choice* are outlined on this Mini Mind Map. Characters and events in the play contribute different ideas about each theme as the play unfolds. Test yourself by copying the Mini Mind Map, adding to it, and then comparing your results with the version on p. 34.

Choice or *'Hobson's Choice'*

'Hobson's choice' means having no real choice at all. It is said to originate from the way a livery stable owner called Hobson allocated horses to people who hired them out. The 'choice' of horse they were given was the one nearest the door, or no horse at all. Brighouse was reminded of the phrase when he saw unwilling young men conscripted to fight for France in the First World War.

CHOICES FOR HOBSON?

The most obvious example of 'Hobson's choice' in the play is when Hobson signs over his business on Will's terms, because that is the only way he can get Maggie back to look after him. This is linked with the choice outlined by Doctor MacFarlane: give up alcohol, or die within six months! When Hobson is offered the choice of paying £500 to settle out of court, the only other option would cause him so much shame that even the loss of his daughters is preferable.

These choices are the consequence of foolish choices Hobson made earlier, when he did have real options: he chose to spend his time drinking with his friends; he chose to deny his daughters the opportunity to marry; he chose to raise his belt to Will, rather than welcoming him into the family. Then he chose one drink too many and fell into Beenstock's cellar. Doctor MacFarlane emphasizes the foolish choices Hobson has made: '*a pretty mess you've made of your liberty.*'

CHOICES FOR THE HOBSON SISTERS AND WILL

The theme is further developed to involve other characters. Maggie chooses Will as her husband because at her age he is her *best chance*. Initially he seems to have very little choice about it: Maggie insists. Before the wedding, she gives him a chance to back out, but he chooses to marry her. By the end, Will has become more decisive and makes many choices. Alice and Vickey choose new lives with their husbands over the old life with their father.

Love and marriage

At the heart of this play is the unconventional love story of Will and Maggie. We are encouraged to compare this with the courtship and marriage of Alice and Albert and Vickey and Fred. Other relationships contribute contrasting ideas: Will's engagement to Ada and marriages we only hear discussed by Hobson and Jim Heeler. ✪ What are the pros and cons of each relationship?

MAGGIE AND WILL

Their relationship has unromantic beginnings. Maggie believes that courtship need not precede marriage and ignores the convention that women should be wooed when she forces Will to marry her. Will does not initially seem attracted to Maggie – in fact she scares him half to death! However, there is a good ground for love to grow: he admires her, is grateful to her, and ends Act 1 by expressing commitment to her. His feelings deepen as she sets about his betterment.

At the end of the play, there is no doubt that shared purpose has brought them together and that genuine love and mutual respect will ensure their happiness. Each has helped the other to become a better person. An important element of their stability is that together they achieve financial as well as emotional security – which Will would never have achieved with Ada.

THE OTHER MARRIAGES

Alice and Albert have a conventional romance: Albert is a handsome, well-dressed solicitor. He courts Alice as well as he can without her father's approval. By marrying him she is assured of financial security and improved status. She gains a house in the Crescent, by comparison with Maggie's cellar in Oldfield Road, and she disparages Maggie's second-hand furniture. She gets what she wants but she will never experience a love like that between Maggie and Will.

Vickey and Fred also have their courtship complicated by Hobson's disapproval, but the reason for their attraction is straightforward: looks. His father is a wholesale grocer, so she too is bettering herself, though not as significantly as Alice. By the end of the play, she has *a child on the way*, the conventional fulfilment of marriage. Again, though, she and Fred seem unlikely to share the happiness of Maggie and Will. Fred is so easy-going and Vickey seems capable of walking all over him.

Hobson and Heeler present caricatures of marriage gone sour: the nagging wife and resentful husband – though Hobson declines after his wife's death. All the signs indicate that Albert and Fred are on the way to a marriage like Hobson's. Will, however, who looked most likely to be hen-pecked, ends up with the most equal marriage.

Female emancipation

Equality between the sexes is investigated in all these portrayals of marriage. This is topical because of the issues the suffragette movement publicized (see p. 2). The Hobson sisters represent the difficulties faced by Victorian women when they tried to control their own lives. They show how men, whether father or husband, exercised power over women's destinies.

HOBSON, A FATHER OF DAUGHTERS

The sisters are treated as property by their father; for example he imagines it is for him to decide who they should marry. He pays them nothing, and they have no means of gaining independence other than by marrying well. This prospect is closed to them without his consent and a dowry. Alice and Vickey escape from their father, but only into marriages in which they quickly assume the support roles of wife as ornament and wife as mother.

Maggie is different, challenging stereotypes of male and female roles. She begins by marrying at the late age of 30, defying her father and setting up home without his help. Other plays of the time explore the life of the independent New Woman, but all have heroines from an affluent family background (women more like Mrs Hepworth). That Maggie earns her own financial security through marriage with an equally penniless husband, a loan and sheer hard work makes her very unusual.

EQUAL IN MARRIAGE?

Maggie assumes the conventional male role: she proposes to Will, buys her own ring and carries it to the church. She tutors her less-educated husband; she expects Will to share in the household chores. She forces Albert and Fred to help Will wash the dishes, because they think they are above doing women's work. She is also physically assertive. The scene where she leads him into the bedroom by the ear was almost censored from the first productions of the play because the idea that a woman would behave like that was both outrageous and indecent.

By the end of the play, almost every man has depended on Maggie for something important in his life. Doctor MacFarlane recognizes her power when he prescribes her as treatment for Hobson. Yet, having gained power, Maggie generously gives it back to the most important man in her life, accepting her husband's conventional right to be the dominant partner in marriage. ✪ What do you think of her doing this?

OTHER INEQUALITIES: CLASS, AGE AND NATIONALITY

Attitudes about social class are shown in Hobson's prejudice against Will, and his mistrust of those who make money without hard work, like solicitors. Overall, Brighouse warns us to think about the damage petty snobbery can cause. He also questions the belief that the older generation are superior to the young, suggesting that respect has to be earned by individuals on the basis of their behaviour to each other, just as in relationships between the sexes.

A final prejudice is that based on nationality. Hobson's distrust of anything *foreign* from French fashion to the Scottish Doctor is, however, more a source of humour than a serious questioning of racial prejudice. Brighouse was writing during the First World War when feelings of nationalism and patriotism were encouraged, including local pride, such as Hobson feels for Salford.

Family life

This theme is connected with the theme of love and marriage, since marriage is the basis of family relationships, also with the theme of equality (between the sexes and young and old). The Hobson family gives us the opportunity to think about the rights and duties of parents and children, husbands and wives.

Hobson is a typical Victorian father. He believes he has the right to control his daughters, including the clothes they wear and the company they keep. He regards it as their duty to look after his house, cook for him, and work in his shop unpaid. He seems to think it is generous of him to pay the local draper *£10 a year to dress you proper*, even though it *is good for trade* that they look attractive in the shop. ✪ How do you think he would have treated a son?

The death of Mary Hobson has had a huge impact on the life of this family. Brighouse implies that the mother has the power in a family (for example, the frightening Mrs Figgins!). Jim tells

Hobson that his wife *does the leathering* when his children disobey him and Hobson's main reason for mourning his wife is that his daughters have been more difficult to control since her death. Maggie has had to take over many of her mother's responsibilities, in the home and in the shop. She has also imposed some order on her father's life, curbed his drinking and made sure he eats regularly. This has upset the usual power balance between parent and child and leads to the breakdown of relationships in the Hobson family. As he feels himself losing control, Hobson becomes more authoritarian and unreasonable.

Hobson's need for his daughters' care at the end of the play raises a question: do children, particularly daughters, have a lifelong duty towards their parents? ❂ What do you think yourself about this issue? Alice and Vickey answer with a resounding *no*. Alice's concern is for her life with her husband and Vickey's is focused on the child she is expecting. Yet Brighouse leads us to judge these two women as proud and selfish.

Work and self-improvement

Brighouse's clear message is that hard work leads to success. This theme would be familiar to his audience: Lancashire was transformed by the Industrial Revolution and became a place where work which involved getting your hands dirty (like Will's) could earn great wealth. The Labour Movement and Christian groups promoted progress through education. A book called *Self-Help*, written by Samuel Smiles in 1859, emphasized what was possible if you worked hard to improve yourself. Will Mossop's rise from rags to riches is just such a story.

EFFORT AND EDUCATION

In this play, the people we admire most are those who work hard. Maggie, for example, runs the shop, while her sisters knit and read and her father drinks. She never misses the opportunity to make a sale and she keeps the accounts efficiently. Tubby Wadlow, who also works hard, judges Maggie to be *a marvel*. She is well matched by Will, whose boot-making skills have been gained through his own efforts.

Note that Will has all the tools of his trade and already has the makings of a thriving business before there are even chairs to sit on at Oldfield Road! This couple achieve success as a result of their own efforts, unlike Albert and Fred.

When Will is offered Mrs Hepworth's card, he is hardly able to read at all. He is ignorant because he has never had an education, until Maggie offers him the chance to improve his intellect and he works as hard at this as he does at his practical boot-making business. Even on his wedding night, he practises his writing. By the end of the play, he is confident, articulate and sophisticated – a testament to what education can achieve.

AMBITION

Hard work needs to be channelled to achieve maximum success – as you will find when you revise! It is not luck but Maggie's ambition that ensures that she and Will build themselves a better future. Ada would not have been able to help him, having no ambition, no education and no skills to complement Will's. Before he shared Maggie's vision, Will would not have improved himself. However, once he learns to think ahead, he can see where improvements are necessary in Hobson's shop. He ends the play with his sights set on a business in St Ann's Square – and together he and Maggie are quite capable of achieving that.

Alcohol and self-destruction

Hobson's alcoholism is the cause of his downfall. The effects of *the demon drink* on his family life, his business and his health drive the plot of *Hobson's Choice*. This theme is the opposite of the self-improvement achieved by Will.

Hobson must have worked hard to build up his business, but his wife's death has allowed him to spend too much time in The Moonraker's. He begins the play with a hangover, loses his two best workers when he lashes out at Will in a drunken temper, falls into Beenstock's cellar when drunk, leading to the loss of his other two daughters, and finally suffers a depressive breakdown. By the time Doctor MacFarlane diagnoses

Hobson's alcoholism, Brighouse has shown that drink badly damages both family life and business.

Moonraker's takes its name from a legend about how some foolish men saw the moon reflected in a pond and spent a lot of time attempting to rake it out. The phrase has come to mean daydreaming, or fantasizing about things that will never happen. ✪ How does this relate to Hobson's behaviour?

For Victorian slum-dwellers alchohol was an easy escape. The same religious and political influences which encouraged people to better their lives very strongly discouraged excessive drinking. 'Temperance' was the name adopted by groups who encouraged total abstaining from alcohol (tee-totalism – drinking nothing stronger than tea – as it became known). Manchester was the home of the largest temperance organization, the United Kingdom Alliance, set up in 1853. Hobson comments that he would like his daughters *to wed temperance young men*. Note that at Maggie's wedding party, the only drink is tea, even for the traditional toast to the bride and groom.

Meanness and generosity

Hobson's meanness is obvious when he refuses to let his daughters marry as he is too tight-fisted to give them marriage portions. He pays Will poor wages, considering his talents, and pays his daughters no wages at all. His meanness contributes to his undoing. Maggie bribes him after his fall into Beenstock's cellar, and he ends up paying out dowries after all. The terms on which he invites Maggie and Will back to Hobson's, which he considers *generous*, are laughable, and he ends up effectively signing his business over to Will. ✪ What is your opinion about the consequences of meanness and selfishness?

In sharp contrast is Mrs Hepworth's generosity when she lends Will and Maggie the capital to set up their shop. They appreciate her support and repay the money as soon as they can. Her support extends beyond money to a generosity of spirit. She did not have to praise Will's boots, neither did she have to send Maggie a wedding bouquet. Ripples spread out from generosity and have a positive effect on many lives.

Maggie, too, has a generous spirit: she finds husbands for her sisters on her own wedding day; she educates Will to benefit him; she returns to her father through concern for his well-being. Her generosity brings her the satisfaction of seeing her sisters married, her father in safe hands and her own marriage prospering.

What can you remember?

? Which characters are important in developing themes, and how? Complete the chart on p. 33 with your ideas.

? Take a good look at the complete Mind Map of themes on p. 34, then turn back to the Mini Mind Map on p. 24 and see how you can expand this with symbols, colours and ideas of your own to summarize the themes of *Hobson's Choice*.

When you feel you understand the play's themes, take a well-deserved break before you start to think about its style and structure.

Major characters involved in development of themes

	MAGGIE	WILL	HOBSON
(ring)	Believes courting is a waste of time.		
(symbols)		Accepts Maggie as his teacher as well as his wife.	
(figures)			
(ladder)			
(bottle)		Wedding toast drunk in tea.	
(slipper)			Refuses to pay wages to his daughters
(mouse)	Sees Will as her only chance to marry.		

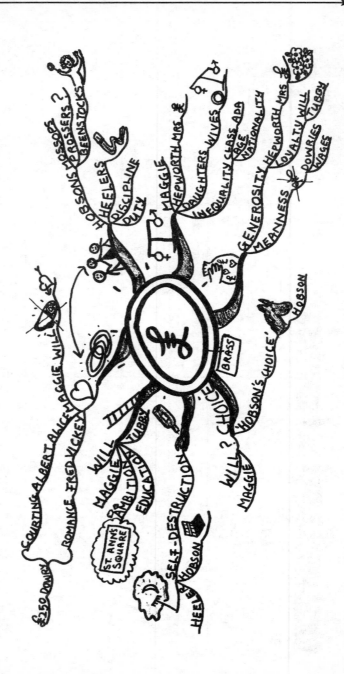

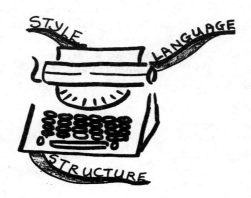

Style, Language and Structure

Making sense of time and place

The new realism in British theatre in the early twentieth century is mirrored in the design of theatre buildings: proscenium arch stages – those like a box fronted with a curtain – are ideal for stage sets which look like a room in someone's home. The curtain swings back to show characters who behave like real people in a realistic setting. They have everyday problems and speak in everyday language. Compare the characters, setting and style of *Hobson's Choice* with a play by Shakespeare.

Lancashire dialect

You cannot fail to notice that almost all of the characters speak with Lancashire accents, most noticeable in the spelling of words spoken by the less-educated characters, for example, *I dunno* for *I don't know*; *what 'ud your father say* for *what would ...*, *axing* for *asking*, and Ada calls Maggie *Miss 'Obson*, without the 'H' sound, which is typical of a Northern English accent.

Some expressions include Lancashire **dialect** words and phrases, not always easily understood by English speakers from other places. Again, the social status of characters is reflected in how frequently their speech deviates from standard English. For example, Mrs Hepworth never uses dialect expressions and Alice and Vickey do so rarely. Hobson and Maggie, however, seem proud to use local speech. There are a couple of occasions where Maggie uses double negatives, considered ungrammatical in standard English; for example, *no use to nobody*. Less-educated characters like Ada and Will are dialect speakers. Will's education includes speaking in formal standard English as well as learning to read and write.

Examples include:

brass (money)	*nay* (no)
come-by-chance (illegitimate child)	*nowt* (nothing)
	nowty (bad-tempered)
Dost ...? (Do you ...?)	*owt* (anything)
fell on rest (died)	*shut of* (rid of)
finicking (fussy)	*Sithee ...* (Look here ...)
gaffer (boss)	*tokened* (engaged to marry)
gradely (good, worthwhile)	*toper* (heavy drinker)
happen (perhaps, maybe)	*victual* (food, feed)
jaw (nag)	*worrits* (worries)
moithered (bothered, confused)	

There are also examples of dialect grammar, where sentences are constructed differently from standard English patterns.
❂ Translate these three examples into standard English, and identify the speaker.

1 *She's golden haired, is Ada.*
2 *You've ate my wedding cake and you've shook my hand.*
3 *Bring your father down and be sharp. I'm busy at my shop, so what they are at his.*

A discussion of dialect would be incomplete without a mention of Doctor MacFarlane and his caricatured Scots speech. He begins merely with the accent, *ma* for *my* and *ye* for *you* but as Hobson angers him he begins to use dialect words and expressions; for example *I ken* for *I know*. Like all the characters in the play, the way he speaks is a part of his personality.

Telling it straight

A characteristic of Lancashire language is plainness of expression. Apart from a few unfamiliar dialect words and some references to people and things that are no longer topical, the language of the play is straightforward and easy to follow. The dialogue imitates spoken English: simple everyday words in short, unadorned sentences. Look at p. 44 in the text (where Hobson knocks on the cellar door and Maggie lets him in, in Act 3). Many of their lines are only three or four words long, often **monosyllables**. ✪ How does this compare with Shakespeare's dialogue?

Fancy speeches and formal words are found mainly in the writing and mouths of lawyers and doctors in this play, a point made by Maggie when she reads Albert's documents and speculates that their *secret language* is a conspiracy to make money.

This sort of down-to-earth common sense is reflected over and over again in the play. A great deal of humour results from the blunt, often cynical, opinions expressed by Maggie, her father and occasionally other characters.

Test yourself

? Where in the play are these lines spoken, and by whom?

'Stiff neck above and weak knees below – it's immodest!'

'They're always out of someone's stock.'

'As plain as Salford Town Hall it's an accident ...'

'Other people's troubles is mostly what folks read the paper for ...'

'Your penny buns'll cost you tuppence now– and more.'

'Ladies that are ladies wants trying on by their own sex, and them that aren't buys clogs.'

'If I'm to be beaten by beer I'll die fighting ...'

'I've had thirty years of the pleasure of living with father, thanks.'

*S*tructure

The **structure** of a play is the way the events of the plot are organized: how the action is divided between the four acts of the play; how within each act events unfold in a sequence of different scenes as characters enter and exit from the stage; how changes of pace build up tension; how the writer manipulates the audience to predict some events, but to be surprised by others, and how and where the climax of each act is placed.

TURNING POINTS

Although the ideas and characters in Brighouse's plays were new and modern, the structure of *Hobson's Choice* is quite traditional. For example, the dramatic climax of each act, involving turning points in Hobson's downfall, is carefully placed to hold the audience's interest: when Hobson beats Will at the end of Act 1, when he storms out towards the end of Act 3 and when Will finally achieves his victory in Act 4. During Act 2, tension is maintained as Maggie's plan is gradually revealed and the audience is drawn into speculation about the possible outcome.

DRAMATIC IRONY

Tension is sometimes created by the technique of **dramatic irony**, where the audience knows more than some of the characters on stage, and is thus encouraged to predict possible outcomes. An example of this is during Act 3 when Alice, Vickey, Albert and Fred are in the next room, unknown to Hobson when he arrives wanting Maggie's advice. As an audience, we anticipate what will happen when they are all brought face to face.

RISE AND FALL

Set against Hobson's 'tragic' downfall (see p. 5), the audience becomes interested in Will's progress. The balance of Hobson's downward journey against Will's upward one is neat and tidy. Visual images emphasize this: the play starts and finishes in Hobson's shop, helping to provide a tight structure. Will makes his first appearance in Act 1 out of the cellar, but his first appearance in Act 4 at the top of a ladder. The **symbolism**, if a little heavy-handed, makes its point. Set against this is Hobson's actual fall, even though it takes place off stage, it is the reverse of Will's first appearance – down into a cellar. By the end, the two men have exchanged appearance, demeanour and role: *'he's the old master, and – ... And you're the new.'*

HUMOUR

Serious messages can have more impact on an audience when they are delivered in an entertaining way. Some of this play's humour is derived from its structure. For example, there are several points where we see **ironic reversal**: Hobson transformed from the tyrant father to a lapdog, because Mrs Hepworth enters the shop; Albert and Fred changed from smart professionals to errand-boy and dish-washer by bossy Maggie; Vickey's change from loving daughter to money-grabbing relative when she finds out how ill her father is. These moments contribute to the exploration of themes such as family life, or social class, as well as revealing character traits. ✪ Can you think of any other examples? Is the effect always humorous?

Humour is also used to manipulate our sympathy for particular characters: it is funny, rather than sad, when Maggie steals Will in a manner Ada describes as *daylight robbery*. Hobson's description of his suicidal thoughts about the razor and shaving water is humorous, not frightening: *question was whether the razor would beat me or I'd beat the razor. I won, that time. The razor's in the yard.* ✪ Take a look at a couple of other moments where humour stops you reacting with sympathy for a character. Which lines make you laugh when Hobson disowns his daughters? And when Hobson finally makes an appearance on stage in Act 4?

What do you think?

? Where would there need to be intervals during a
   production of *Hobson's Choice*? Why? How does the
   structure of the play help build the tension leading up
   to each interval?

? Can you explain four ways that Hobson and Will
   change places, comparing their circumstances at the
   beginning of the play with their circumstances at
   the end?

*Now you have some structure for your
thoughts, take a break before getting down
to detail.*

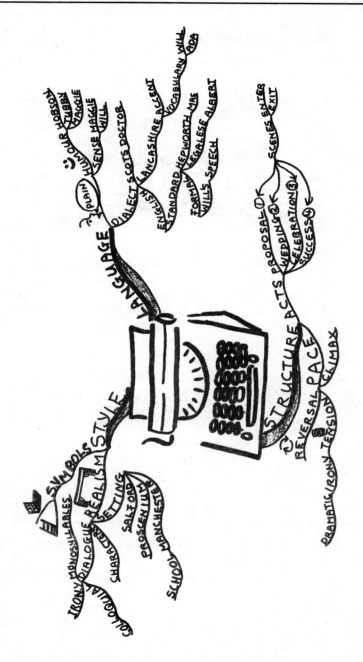

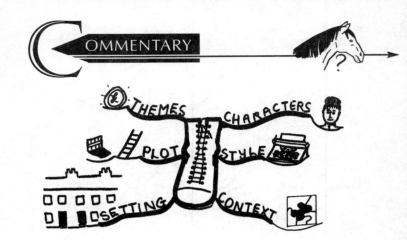

COMMENTARY

The Commentary divides the play into short sections, beginning with a brief preview which will prepare you for the section and help in last-minute revision. It comments on whatever is important in the section, focusing on the areas shown in the Mini Mind Map above.

ICONS

Wherever there is a focus on a particular theme, the icon for that theme appears in the margin (see p. x for key). Look out, too, for the 'Style and language' icons. Being able to comment on style and language will help you to get an 'A' in your exam.

You will learn more from the Commentary if you use it alongside the play itself. Read a section from the play, then the corresponding Commentary section – or the other way around.

QUESTIONS

Remember that when a question appears in the Commentary with a star ✪ in front of it, you should stop and think about it for a moment. And **remember to take a break** after completing each exercise!

Act 1, *Proposal (pp. 1–25)*

◆ Stage setting: time, place and the Hobson sisters.
◆ Albert Prosser – the reluctant customer.
◆ Henry Hobson – tyrant and Victorian father.
◆ Mrs Hepworth praises Will Mossop's boots.
◆ Hobson asks for Jim Heeler's advice.
◆ Maggie proposes marriage to Will.
◆ Maggie overcomes Will's objections to her proposal.
◆ The Hobsons react to news of Maggie's marriage plans.
◆ Will stands up to Hobson.

THE STAGE SET (P. 1)

Each act opens with a detailed description of the stage setting. Imagine you are in the audience in a theatre. ○ What do you learn about the place, the time and the people?

Place: the action takes place in a shoe shop, which is also a home. The shop looks *dingy but business-like*, so you may judge that the shop is busy but not 'posh'. The clogs in the window hint at the usual customers – working people employed in the mines and textile mills wore clogs. The set would not tell you this was Salford, but a local audience would quickly work it out from the accents of the characters and place names like Chapel Street and Hope Hall.

Time: this is in the nineteenth century. The style of boots and the gas lights are clues, as are the costumes and hairstyles of the characters on stage, with their long skirts and shop aprons. The bright light shining through the window shows it is midday and Alice's comment that Hobson is late leaving hints that Hobson regularly goes drinking before lunch

The characters: the first thing you notice about Alice and Vickey is that, even in their plain working clothes, they are stylish. Vickey, in particular, is very pretty. Although they are at work, during this slack moment in the shop, Alice is knitting and Vickey is reading. The contrast with Maggie is immediate. Her costume is less fashionable than theirs, plainer, older – like Maggie herself! And what Maggie does the minute she walks on stage is also a contrast: she sets to work, at the desk, with the shop's account book.

❂ You might like to sketch designs for the sisters' costumes for Act 1. Compare these with costumes they wear later in the play. What aspects of their characters are reinforced by the way they dress?

ALBERT PROSSER – THE RELUCTANT CUSTOMER (PP. 1–4)

The sisters' discussion about their father's night out at a Masons' meeting (see below) and his need for *reviving* this morning is interrupted by a visit from Albert Prosser, the young man who is courting Alice. Maggie's reaction is immediate: she sells him a pair of expensive boots and arranges for his old pair to be mended and sent round to his house with the bill. She says she's *sick of the sight* of him and Alice courting in the shop. In her opinion, he should just get on and marry her, if that is what they both want. '*Courting must come first*' Alice protests; in answer, Maggie picks up a fancy slipper likening it to courtship: '*all glitter and no use to nobody.*'

We begin to build up a picture of family life in this household. In the absence of a mother, Hobson seems to be an over-protective father, to say the least. He has forbidden his daughters to have boyfriends and Alice seems nervous of Albert being found in the shop at all. ❂ Is Maggie as the eldest of the three girls, her father's second in command? Or are her words and actions more like those of a substitute mother for her sisters?

HENRY HOBSON – TYRANT AND VICTORIAN FATHER (PP. 5–8)

We begin to get the measure of Hobson from the moment he first walks on the stage. His clothes tell us he is a man who is successful in his business, rather than a gentleman. He belongs to the Freemasons: we know he was at a Masons' meeting the night before, and he has masonic emblems on his watch chain. Note that the Masons is a male-only organization, and it seems fair to say that Hobson is a man's man, most comfortable in the company of other businessmen like himself. As a parent, he likes to feel he is in control of his three daughters (his *rebellious females* who have become *uppish* since their mother died). He tells them that he does not appreciate their attempts to control his coming and going. He calls their attitude *bumptious* (meaning vain, conceited) and makes a comment to remember later: *I hate bumptiousness like I hate a lawyer*.

He criticizes his younger daughters for *dress[ing] up like guys*, making a spectacle of themselves by wearing dresses with bustles (*a hump added to nature*) which he dislikes not so much because they are fashionable as because his daughters are imitating the dress of the upper classes, or looking *like French madams*. The lack of logic in this remark is typical of Hobson's emotional response to events!

His tirade reaches a climax as he threatens to choose a husband for each of the girls. Alice and Maggie both protest: Alice at not having any say about her own husband; Maggie because her father dismisses out of hand her chances of marriage, saying that, at 30, she is past the marrying age. As a shrewd businessman he must also know that Maggie, who runs his shop very efficiently for no wages at all whilst he drinks with his friends, is too valuable to lose.

❍ Who gains your sympathy during this family argument? Is it Hobson, coping with his rebellious girls with no wife to help him out? Is it Vickey and Alice, with their father's interference in their clothing and their lives? Is it Maggie, with her father's mockery of her marriage chances?

MRS HEPWORTH PRAISES WILL MOSSOP'S BOOTS (PP. 8–11)

Hobson's manner changes completely when Mrs Hepworth's carriage stops outside and she enters the shop. He is servile and ingratiating to his wealthy customer. He assumes she has come to complain when she asks Tubby Wadlow who made the boots she is wearing. Tubby calls Will Mossop up from the workshop in the cellar and we form our first impressions of this poorly dressed, timid man who cringes as if Mrs Hepworth is about to hit her when she hands him her visiting card with the words '*Take that.*' He is so ill-educated that he can barely read the words on the card.

It is a surprise to both Will and Hobson that Mrs Hepworth praises Will for *the best made pair of boots I've ever had*. However Hobson's meanness contrasts with her generous praise: when she suggests that Will is probably underpaid, Hobson sends him back to the cellar straight away. Hobson's reaction to her visit is, typically, illogical. He is annoyed that Will has been praised because he may want a pay rise and says he does not want further custom from Mrs Hepworth. However, he is quite happy to boast to his friend Jim Heeler that Mrs Hepworth and her family are *old and valued customers*. ✪ How does Maggie's reaction to Mrs Hepworth contrast with her father's? What do you think Maggie might decide to do next? Why?

HOBSON ASKS JIM HEELER'S ADVICE (PP. 11–14)

Hobson surprises Jim Heeler, a local grocer, by delaying their usual lunchtime visit to The Moonraker's. He wants to talk to him privately about the trouble he is having with his daughters, not in front of their drinking companions Sam Minns, the pub landlord, Denton and Tudsbury, the draper. Jim claims his own daughters are generally obedient, or *the missus does the leathering*. Their discussion implies that family relationships involve power struggles: the parents' generation have the right to beat the children into submission; likewise, the husband attempts to keep his wife under his control. Hobson moans that since his wife died, he is now dominated by three women instead of just one.

The suffragette movement (see p. 2) gives topical significance to Jim Heeler's remark about *women ... getting above themselves*. The two men discuss the difficulty they experience in subduing their womenfolk. Hobson says that *roaring* (shouting) at them has not had any effect. Jim's advice is to get them married – presumably to pass the problem of dealing with their disobedience to some other man. Hobson's wish to find them *temperance young men* (abstainers from alcohol) leads Jim Heeler to remark that such desirable husbands will cost Hobson substantial amounts of money in marriage settlements for his daughters. He compares this to baiting a hook to catch fish.

Hobson has already declared that *Maggie's too useful to part with* in the shop. When he realizes it will cost money to marry off Alice and Vickey he changes his mind. His daughters only cost him their keep: he is too mean to pay them wages for their work, though possibly this is justified in Vickey and Alice's case! Hobson's solution to is to *forget there's such a thing as women in the world* by joining his circle of male friends in The Moonraker's. Ironically, his claim to be master in his own home is undermined as Maggie reminds him, two times more, that he must be back for his dinner at one o'clock.

What can you remember?

? Make a list of the names of all the characters you have seen, or heard mentioned, so far. How many of their occupations do you know? (You should have 12 names in a complete list.)

? In which ways is Maggie different from her two sisters? Jot down all the contrasts you can think of, maybe around the costume designs you did at the beginning of this scene.

? How many times did you notice Hobson react to events in a way that was impetuous, illogical or confused? Do you think this is an aspect of his character? Or can you think of another explanation for his erratic words and behaviour?

? What have you learned about Will Mossop so far? Begin a Mind Map to note down his deficiencies and his talents.

Now take a break, before you read on ... and prepare yourself for a surprise!

MAGGIE PROPOSES MARRIAGE TO WILL (PP. 14–16)

Two things influence Maggie to act as she does next. One is her father's firm belief that she is too old to marry. The other is Mrs Hepworth's praise of Will's talents. She calls Will up from the cellar. His reluctance and nervousness is plain, especially when she takes his hands and compliments him on their extraordinary skill: since his only training has been at Hobson's, she concludes he must be a *natural born genius* as a bootmaker. She echoes Mrs Hepworth's words as she asks Will when he will leave Hobson's, saying he is a fool to pass up the opportunity of earning much higher wages in Manchester. She asks him a leading question: does he stay at Hobson's because he likes the people? His simple nature shows as he says he would be afraid to go in a big shop and he completely misses her heavy hints, saying he does not really know why he stays, other that than he is *used to* Hobson's.

Maggie tries again to prompt Will to speak. She points out that they are *a pair* in the sense that his skills in the workshop and her skills as a saleswoman are what keep the business going. He is still completely oblivious to what she is trying to get him to say and she has to stop him returning to work by being even more obvious. She says she has been watching Will for a long time: for six months she has been certain he is the one for her. He is astonished as the meaning of her words becomes clear. She tells him that his hands and her business sense make them a natural *working partnership*. He expresses relief: a partnership is *a different thing* when he thought she was asking him to marry her. Now he has said the word, Maggie can be completely direct. *I am*, she says bluntly. ✪ Is Maggie reacting to events as emotionally and impetuously as her father during this conversation? What reasons do you have for your opinion?

✪ What exactly is she proposing to Will? Is it a business arrangement? Or does she want more than a marriage of convenience? What do you think of the way she goes about asking him to marry her?

MAGGIE OVERCOMES ALL WILL'S OBJECTIONS (PP. 16–21)

Will gives Maggie a string of reasons why marriage is not a possibility. He begins by reminding the audience that she is *the master's daughter*. She is superior in education and social status. Maggie brushes this off: she wants a man who is different from her father (and Will certainly is) and she sees Will as her *best chance*. At her age, with her possessive father and considering the people she is likely to meet in a Salford shoe shop, she has made the only practical choice. Will says that, though he respects and admires her he is *none in love* with her and that a marriage with no love stands little chance of success. She dismisses this saying she has *the love all right*. Will's fears about Hobson's reaction to the news are his next objection. Maggie agrees that *he'll say a lot*, but that does not deter her. Clearly, so far, she has thought through all these points herself.

Will's next objection is a surprise: he says he is already engaged (*tokened*). Maggie has seen this Ada Figgins and her assessment is dismissive: Ada is *helpless* and trusts Will *to make the future right*. Together, they are destined for a life of poverty: Ada could not help Will move beyond his job as an *eighteen shilling a week bootmaker*. When Ada enters, the outcome of her discussion with Maggie is a foregone conclusion. Ada says she loves him because he plays the jew's harp (not the most useful accomplishment in the world!). She has no plans for their future, seeing this as Will's responsibility; a direct contrast with Maggie. She puts up little resistance when Maggie tells the pair of them Will is to marry her, not Ada. She offers to sell Ada a pair of clogs, then tells her to leave.

The final obstacle in Will's mind is Ada's mother: Will fears her nagging when he returns home. Maggie realizes that Mrs Figgins has decided Will should marry Ada and finds a quick solution. He will move from the Figgins' and lodge with Tubby Wadlow until they marry. Will's relief is evident: '*it's like an 'appy dream,*' he says. However, her suggestion that he can now organize the marriage ceremony in the minimum three weeks' time it takes for the banns to be displayed outside the church is met by as much fear as her suggestion that he should now kiss her. ✪ Do you think marriage to Maggie is likely to be happier for Will than marriage to Ada? Why? In what ways does Maggie defy conventional ideas about how a woman should behave both in proposing to Will and in reorganizing his life? What aspects of Will's behaviour are not what you would expect of a stereotypical male?

THE HOBSONS REACT TO MAGGIE'S NEWS (PP. 21–4)

Alice and Vickey give Will an excuse to dive back down the cellar. More objections to the marriage come from Alice, who emphasizes the social difference between the couple and how this will reduce the respectability of the family. She does not want Will as a brother-in-law. She knows their father will object. She even fears for her chances with Albert Prosser.

Hobson returns from The Moonraker's and Vickey hints at Maggie's news strongly enough to force Maggie to tell him outright that she is to marry Will. Hobson reacts emotionally and illogically: she is too old; he is the one who will choose husbands, though *there will be no husbands here*. He sends his daughters out to the living room to serve his lunch (which he calls *dinner* in the way of the North of England), but Maggie stands up to him. She is not impressed by his reminding her that Will's father was illegitimate, *a come-by chance*, and that she will make him *a laughing stock* in the area if he agrees to the marriage.

Maggie's determination is unshaken. She tells her father that from now on she expects to be paid 15 shillings a week and threatens the alternative that she and Will leave. This is the final straw for her mean father. He says, impetuously, he can replace shop hands cheaply, a foolish comment considering the talents Will and Maggie would take away from his business.

✪ Do you have any sympathy with any of Alice's or Hobson's objections to Will as a member of their family?

WILL STANDS UP TO HOBSON (PP. 24–5)

Enraged by Maggie's demands, Hobson calls for Will. He wants to vent his anger by taking his belt to someone, and females are not appropriate. He threatens to *beat the love* from Will's body every morning till he gives Maggie up. Will's reaction is a complete surprise. He stands up to Hobson, saying that he is not the one who is chasing Maggie, but one touch of the leather belt will be enough for him to change his mind. Hobson hits him and Will is as good as his word. He kisses Maggie and promises that any further use of the belt will leave the couple no alternative but to *walk straight out of shop* to start their own business. Maggie is proud and delighted. Will seems shell-shocked once his anger subsides. Hobson is as amazed as the audience.

Think about it

?   Who is Ada Figgins? Why would she have made a most unsuitable wife for Will Mossop?

?   List the objections Will makes to the idea of marriage with Maggie. List the objections Hobson and Alice make to the proposed marriage. Can you see any similarities between the two lists?

?   Remind yourself of the meaning of the expression 'Hobson's choice' (p. 24) Which characters make a 'choice' during Act 1 because there is no realistic alternative?

?   What further aspects of Will Mossop's character are you able to add to your Mind Map after his second (pp. 14–21) and third (pp. 24–5) appearances on stage?

Break for refreshments during the interval, before you find out how Will Mossop keeps his promise.

Act 2, *Wedding (pp. 26–38)*

◆ Stage setting: changes in Hobson's shop.
◆ Alice and Vickey are not coping with business.
◆ Maggie gets a husband for herself – and her sisters.
◆ A brass wedding ring and second-hand furniture.
◆ Albert and Freddie repay Maggie for their improved wedding prospects.
◆ Will, the bridegroom.

THE STAGE SET (P. 26)

Place: The setting is described briefly, as this Act is also in Hobson's shop.

Time: It is again mid-day, but the script tells us it is a month later. Clues are there that time has passed and that changes have occurred.

The characters: We soon discover that Maggie and Will have left Hobson's. One obvious clue is that Alice is sitting at Maggie's desk looking at the account books. Tubby, instead of being at work in the workshop, is standing with her. Vickey, though, is reading as she was at the opening of Act 1.

○ Imagine that you are the stage manager of a production. What kind of book would you give Vickey to read? How could the setting reflect the impact of Maggie and Will's departure? Would the display of shoes and clogs on the shelves look different? How could you make the shop look less tidy, less orderly, less busy? Vickey says, *'it's all at sixes and sevens'*: how could you show this?

ALICE AND VICKEY ARE NOT COPING (PP. 26–8)

Alice and Tubby discuss problems in the shop: there is no work to do in the workshop because few sales are being made and orders for shoes are not coming in. Tubby says, *'the high-class trade has dropped like a stone.'* Hobson is not there to tell Tubby what to do. Alice is not able to make any sort of decision. She simply agrees when Tubby suggests making more clogs to add to the shop's stock, even though this is a bad use of time. Tubby points out the price of clogs is not enough to pay the rent, let alone his wages. The cause for the changes, both the decline in business and Hobson's increasingly bad temper is that Maggie and Will have left.

Maggie is sadly missed: first because she was able to manage the business without her father, to give Tubby his orders and to balance the books, unlike Alice who accepts Vickey's wrong total of 17 and 25 to make 52 – check it yourself! Second, Hobson is wasting more time in The Moonraker's, now that Maggie no longer keeps him under control. Will's departure has also contributed to loss of sales, as customers who can afford high-quality footwear no longer shop at Hobson's. ✪ Think back to Will's threat to Hobson. What must have happened, and what does it show you about Will's character that he kept his word?

MAGGIE GETS A HUSBAND FOR HERSELF – AND FOR HER SISTERS (PP. 27–32)

Alice moans about doing the accounts and wishes she was *married and out of it*. Vickey hints that she, too, dreams of marriage, but has not bothered to discuss her young man with Alice because Maggie's engagement to Will has spoiled their *chances for ever*. There are two ways this could be interpreted. First, Maggie's rebellion against her father will have made him stricter still with the two younger daughters. Second, Vickey's snobbishness shows when she blames Will, saying that nobody would want him for a brother-in-law. This echoes Alice's earlier objections and reminds us of Hobson's description of Will's humble origins.

Maggie and Will enter with Fred Beenstock. We have not met this smartly dressed young man before, but we quickly discover he is Vickey's boyfriend. Maggie hints that she intends to help both her sisters to change Hobson's mind about their forbidden romances, as they seem likely to *never get no farther with it* without her intervention. Maggie's offer to help seems the more extraordinary when we discover that this is her and Will's wedding day. She sends Fred to collect Albert from the solicitor's office, with orders to *bring the paper*. It becomes clear later that this paper is a legal writ. Alice worries about their father's reaction when he returns to find two young men in his shop. Maggie knows this will not happen.

The reason for Maggie's confidence is that Hobson has fallen through an open trap door into the cellar warehouse of Beenstock's grocery business. Fred euphemistically says that Hobson *wasn't looking very carefully where he was going.* The description of him, sound asleep on some bags of flour and *snoring very loudly,* indicates that he was drunk. Maggie's sarcastic comment that her sisters *must have worried father very badly* to cause such reckless behaviour reminds us how rapidly both the man and his business have gone downhill and that Hobson's intemperance has been the cause.

Maggie's plan to get her sisters married is hinted at. She points out that their father threatened to choose husbands for her sisters and she does not *allow for folks to change their minds.* ❂ How does Hobson's present plight enable Alice and Vickey to marry?

Vickey reminds Maggie that her rebellion against their father's decision that Maggie should remain unmarried has not made it any easier for her sisters to make any progress in that direction. This leads to discussion about Will, who Maggie insists must now be welcomed as a member of the family with no more argument about it. After all, he is now socially their superior as master of his own business, since they are just shop assistants.

Maggie emphasizes how the business she and Will have set up has improved Will's status. He is no longer *Willie Mossop ... boothand* but *William Mossop, Practical boot and shoe maker* and he has his own business cards to prove it. ❂ Can he read these any better than he read Mrs Hepworth's card in Act 1? Will, according to Maggie, is now his own master. He qualifies this with a witty remark that although he has his *name wrote up on the windows,* he has some doubts about *being master.* Her sisters are privileged to be able to call him by his first name rather than Mr Mossop.

Someone has agreed to invest capital into the business. We are reminded of the partnership Maggie suggested to Will. Her business sense has made this happen, but his skills are crucial to the success of the enterprise. Neither of them could have started up a business alone. ❂ Who do you think would be able and willing to put finance behind this winning combination of talents?

Maggie has come down in the world, moving from her father's comfortable home in Chapel Street to Oldfield Road, a less affluent area. The address, 39a, hints that it is not even a whole house. But her pride in Will's self-improvement, which she has made possible, is unmistakable. Her ambition for future success is hinted at when she refuses to help Alice with Hobson's accounts, pointing out that Mossop's is *a rival shop*. Maggie remarks knowingly that there is not so much *high-class trade* keeping Hobson's shop so busy that her sisters have not the time to come along to St Philip's Church to see her and Will marry.

A BRASS WEDDING RING AND SECOND-HAND FURNITURE (PP. 32–5)

Maggie's practical, unromantic approach to marriage is emphasized as she buys a fourpenny brass shoe-ring to use as a wedding ring. Maggie's practicality extends to her home. Her sisters are horrified to find out that she and Will are to set up home in a cellar dwelling, the cheapest housing available. Furthermore, she has bought furniture second hand. Maggie's comment that Vickey would want a *semi-detached and a houseful of new furniture* is echoed by Vickey herself: '*I'd start properly or not at all.*' ○ Maggie says: '*When folks can't afford the best, they have to do without.*' But she and Will have been given money. What have they spent it on instead of a better home and new furniture? Do you agree with Vickey about starting married life *properly*?

ALBERT AND FRED REPAY MAGGIE FOR THEIR IMPROVED WEDDING PROSPECTS (PP. 35–7)

Maggie demonstrates that she is in charge of the future life of every man on stage. She reminds her sisters that she has a plan to get them married with the expected dowry (*marriage portions*) from their father. When Fred returns with Albert Prosser, Maggie sends her sisters away so she can discuss business. But first, she establishes firmly who is in control by ordering stylishly dressed Fred to get his jacket off and help Will bring a broken sofa down from the attic.

Alone with Albert, she reads through the *blue paper* he has brought. This is written in *legal English*, full of words like *to wit* and *whereas*. Maggie shares her father's lack of trust of lawyers, seeing the use of a *secret language* which is definitely *not the sort we speak in Lancashire*, as a conspiracy between professional people. Albert proves the point as he 'translates' the document and Maggie's plan takes shape.

Fred has instructed Albert to sue Hobson on three counts: trespass, damage and spying on trade secrets. Albert is worried that the action would not stand up to much investigation, but Maggie assures him that her father's hatred of the legal profession should ensure that he will wish to settle this business swiftly and privately. She tells Fred to put the document on top of her father so he will see it when he awakes. It becomes obvious that bribery is part of her plan.

Her final order is to remind Albert not to get above himself. He might be a fashionable young solicitor, but she has done him a favour and he has to pay, too. His task is to push the hand-cart full of broken furniture through the streets to the cellar in Oldfield Road at the risk of being seen by his friends. In a way this is a test: if he won't do it, he is too proud to make a good husband for Alice. ✪ What does it tell you about Maggie that she spends so much time thinking about the future happiness of others on her own wedding day?

Maggie's cynical comments about the 'legalese' of the document and her comparison of it to doctors' use of Latin on prescriptions highlights the style of writing of the dialogue in the play. Lancashire people pride themselves on being plain-spoken, down to earth and saying bluntly what they mean. Maggie and Hobson both share this way of speaking and, with it, a dislike of airs and graces of any kind – in language, dress, attitude or behaviour. ✪ How many examples can you think of in the play so far?

WILL, THE BRIDEGROOM (P. 38)

Maggie has dominated Act 2, ordering everyone about and organizing every little detail. She turns to Will as they are about to set off to the church to ask him how he feels, saying that this is not a visit to the dentist to be endured, but a

place where he must answer truthfully when asked by the vicar if he will take her as his wife. Will is under no illusions: he wryly remarks, in contrast to the dentist where you *get rid of summat*, getting married is about taking on responsibilities.
❂ Where else have you seen evidence of Will's quick wit and sense of humour?

He is entering into marriage by free choice, unlike most others in this scene who do what Maggie tells them; as he puts it, affectionately, '*You're growing on me lass.*' Maggie's remark to Vickey that she has the ring because she couldn't trust Will to remember it comes across more as a fond joke than a criticism. Their relationship is moving into a new closeness, and there are signs that Will is becoming more of an equal partner.
❂ Where else in Act 2 was there evidence of this?

As they leave for the church, Tubby throws old shoes after them, a traditional way of wishing newly-weds good luck, but particularly suited to those in the shoe-making business!

Test yourself

?   What has happened to business at Hobson's and to Hobson himself? What is the main cause of the changes since Act 1?

?   What four things does Maggie take away from the shop that she did not arrive with? What do we learn about Alice and Vickey from their opinion about each of these?

?   What are the family businesses of Alice and Vickey's boyfriends? How do these combine to make Maggie's plan possible?

?   What are the three charges Hobson is accused of, and why would they be unlikely to stand up in a court of law?

Now take a break before you join the wedding celebrations.

Act 3, *Celebration (pp. 39–59)*

- Stage setting: the cellar in Oldfield Road.
- Will makes a speech.
- The men wash the dishes.
- Hobson asks for Maggie's help.
- Will speaks what comes into his mind.
- Hobson settles out of court.
- Hobson disowns his daughters.
- Will's education continues.

THE STAGE SET (P. 39)

Place: The setting is Will and Maggie's new home: *two cellars on Oldfield Road*. We see the *room to live and work in*, the bedroom is indicated by a door. Lettering on the windows shows the business's name: *William Mossop, Practical Bootmaker*. The sparse furnishings indicate Will and Maggie's spending priorities, the equipment of Will's trade is all there: a bench to work on, leather and tools. Home comforts are limited to a screen to hide the sink, a cupboard and a table, presumably purchases from the Flat Iron Market. The chairs and sofa from Hobson's provide the only seating. Maggie and Will must have been too busy to sit down until today! Note that the chairs have already been mended. On the table are the remains of their 'wedding feast'. There has been a celebration, but no great outlay of money. There is a teapot (the only drink – no alcohol), slices from *a large pork pie and a small wedding cake*. One bright item catches the eye in this dark, shabby room: a bouquet of expensive hot-house flowers on the table. ✪ Who do you think sent these?

The characters: Vickey, Alice and their young men drink a toast to the bride and groom, from tea-cups. Maggie and Will are seated on the two chairs.

Time: It is the evening after the wedding. A street lamp shining through the window indicates the time of day.

WILL MAKES A SPEECH (PP. 39–41)

Maggie's influence has already changed Will considerably. This shows as he makes the bridegroom's speech. He is quite nervous and when he forgets his words, Maggie prompts him. Obviously, she has rehearsed with him what he should say, but his progress shows in how this one-time tongue-tied, ill-educated man now uses formal words such as *sentiments so cordially expressed* as he proudly offers a toast to his guests.

Alice is surprised enough to curtail Albert's attempt to reply saying '*you'll not speak as well as he did,*' and Albert is a solicitor who speaks in public as part of his job! Vickey asks who taught Will to speak. The provider of his education in speech making, as many other things, is Maggie. She expresses confidence in her pupil's continuing progress: '*in another twenty years ... I know which of you three men'll be thought most of at the Bank.*' Hard work has set Will off on the path to self-improvement. He has grown in self-confidence and social skills.

He has also gained the backing of an affluent patron, for Will could not have saved enough from his meagre wages at Hobson's to finance this venture. Maggie will only reveal that there has been help from the person who sent the flowers for her bridal bouquet. Mrs Hepworth's praise of Maggie's good sense and Will's craftsmanship is worth remembering. ✪ How else might she have helped them, as well as investing money in their business?

THE MEN WASH THE DISHES (PP. 41–3)

The reversal of expected male and female roles between Will and Maggie is exploited for comic purposes. It is unusual for a man to admit to being educated by his wife, but Will's instant obedience when Maggie tells him to clear the table provokes laughter from Freddie and Albert. Maggie teaches them a lesson by telling them to *lend ... a hand with the washing-up.* That they ask for Will's opinion whether they should comply shows growing respect for him. He is unashamed to tell them that the table needs clearing for his lessons. Humour also follows from Will's admission that he is reluctant to see them leave because he has never been alone with Maggie and he is, as Freddie guesses, *shy of his wife.*

The conversation has echoes of an innocent, young bride confiding in her close female friends, especially as the three men are busy with trays of pots and tea towels.

The humour still works nearly a hundred years later. Maggie reinforces the point that these fine young men are no better than Will, and that no man should consider himself so superior to women that he is above doing his share of household chores. ✪ Are some gender stereotypes as ingrained in our attitudes as they were at the beginning of the twentieth century? Do you think Maggie's lesson in equality is still relevant today?

HOBSON ASKS FOR MAGGIE'S HELP (PP. 44–8)

A knock at the door turns out to be Henry Hobson: finding himself in deep trouble he comes to Maggie for help. Of course, he is unaware that it is her wedding day, or that he is about to walk into a family celebration, let alone the extent of his family's involvement in his trouble!

Brighouse makes use of dramatic irony here: the theatre audience knows more about the situation than most of the characters on stage. ✪ Which character has the fullest understanding of what is likely to happen? How many times can you spot dramatic irony in the events that follow?

Maggie sends her sisters and their young men into the bedroom, implying that they will come out again before Hobson has left, despite their reluctance to see him. She then reminds Will that he is *gaffer* and initially, to Hobson's amazement, refuses to let him in until she has *ask[ed] the master*. Will slips into this role with similar confidence to that shown when he delivered his speech; also, he is relieved to postpone the moment he will be alone with Maggie and expresses the hope that Hobson will stay *a good long while*.

Maggie seizes the opportunity to add to her father's anguish. He is suffering from a hangover, so when she offers him a cup of stewed tea, some pork-pie and a slice of wedding cake, it provokes amusing groans and shudders from Hobson, especially when she forces him to eat the cake. Finally, she allows him to tell her the reason for his visit.

Upon hearing he is in trouble, she stands to leave the room, turning her father's views back on him: *'Women are only in your way.'* Such matters only concern men. He begs her to stay and listen and produces the summons. Maggie gives it to Will, who holds it upside down. Clearly, his reading still has room for improvement! Hobson hardly notices: he is beside himself with fear and hurt pride. His status in the area will suffer from having a legal action against him. He is widely respected as a warden at the local church, a businessman and an upright family man.

When Maggie asks him the plain question *'Did you trespass?'* he has to admit the truth the audience has already guessed. He *stayed too long* in The Moonraker's. He tries to make Maggie feel guilty, blaming his drunkenness on her departure. The accident has led to his worst nightmare, combining lawyers and spending money (both of which he hates) with the loss of his reputation in the neighbourhood. He knows that a public court case where he admits to being drunk at mid-day will lose the few respectable customers Hobson's has left. ❏ Do you feel sorry for Hobson at this point, or do you think he deserves what has happened?

More questions to think about

? Identify three occasions so far when Maggie encourages Will to behave like the master of his own home.

? What does Maggie offer her father to eat and drink, and why is it amusing?

? What has this Act shown about men's expectations of women? Can you think of two occasions where Maggie has forced them to question the usual stereotypes?

? What are three main reasons why Hobson does not want to appear before a court of law?

Now take a short break before you see Hobson get several nasty surprises.

WILL SPEAKS WHAT COMES INTO HIS MIND (PP. 48–50)

Hobson explains his distrust of the legal profession. His comments echo Maggie's cynical reaction to legal English. He says lawyers are able to twist the way ideas are expressed to *make white show as black*. Plain speech which says honestly what it means is part of the Salford character. Fancy talk, like fancy clothes and fancy ways, is foreign and not to be trusted. This idea is repeated at various points in the play. ✪ When else have you heard characters express a similar opinion? Which characters?

Will's comments show how education has sharpened his wit as well as his conversational skills. When Hobson laments that lawyers will *squeeze him dry* over this case, Will picks up the sense of *dry* meaning sober, or not full of drink, and jokes, '*that's summat like a squeeze.*' Will's enquiry about whether the newspaper will report the incident adds to Hobson's worries, for he fears that not only the local paper will carry the story, but for a man of his status, the daily newspaper *The Manchester Guardian*, will spread publicity to *the whole of Lancashire*.

Will's naivity shows when he says that it would be almost worth having your reputation ruined to read about yourself. When Hobson points out that other people also have that pleasure, Will speculates that people do like to read about misfortunes, especially when they know the person involved. Though true, this is hardly a tactful thing to say to Hobson at this moment! Will then gives advice, with well-chosen examples, of the benefits of expecting the worst possible outcome, so that Hobson will experience no further unpleasant surprises. Will underestimates his progress when he describes himself as *not much good at talking*! ✪ What does this conversation show us about Will's education and his developing powers of thought and understanding? (Notice, though, that he is aware of his limitations and leaves the legal negotiations with Albert completely to Maggie.)

HOBSON SETTLES OUT OF COURT (PP. 50–5)

Maggie tells her father that if publicity is what alarms him, then the only solution is to settle out of court. He has no choice. Hobson's dislike of lawyers and his meanness with money show again as he speculates that *behind closed doors* in their offices, lawyers probably *squeeze twice as hard* as they would dare in a public court. He fears this solution will *cost a fortune.*

Albert is summoned and Hobson is disgusted to discover *one so young* is a lawyer, presumably feeling it should take a long time to learn such evil ways. He is astonished to see his younger daughters enter, along with *Mr Beenstock, of Beenstock and Co.*, but his astonishment turns to anger when it occurs to him that Tubby has been left in charge of the shop. Having lost control of his business, he is even more determined to control his daughters. When Maggie says she and Will would return the compliment and close their shop to go to her sisters' weddings, Hobson explodes, '*it'll be many a year before there's another wedding in this family.*'

When Albert refers to the *business* they need to attend to, Hobson's rage is turned on to him: '*Honest men live by business and lawyers live by law.*' Albert adds libel to the list of charges, since this comment implies that there is some dishonesty involved. Albert's deft turning of Hobson's every word against him shows that he is right to distrust fine-sounding talk. When Albert explains that the damages awarded in court would be even higher than settling in private, Hobson cuts him short with the blunt question: '*How much?*'

Albert greedily suggests £1,000. Maggie does not want to see her father exploited so she says Hobson could sue Beenstock's for causing the accident by leaving the trap-door open and suggests a sum she knows he can afford: £500. She has done his accounts for long enough to base the amount on knowledge. Hobson is appalled at the idea of parting even with £500, until Vickey suggests that he has beaten the law by paying half what was asked. Hobson's relief is short lived: Maggie tells him the money is not *going out of the family*, because it will be split between Alice and Vickey as marriage portions. Each now has a dowry of £250. ✪ Do you feel sorry for Hobson, or do you feel he deserved this trick to be played on him?

HOBSON DISOWNS HIS DAUGHTERS (PP. 55–7)

Irrationally, the enraged Hobson casts off his family ties and makes his most foolish decision when he says that from now on he will *run that shop with men*. There will be no welcome for the girls if they ever want to come back. As he leaves, he says that Will, as an honest tradesman, is now the only one of the six he has any time for. Both these comments point, ironically, to the events of Act 4.

He states that, unlike the three young men, he is free of women's control over his life. It is obvious that without the structure his daughters gave to his home life, the downfall of Hobson and his business will continue even more rapidly. When Freddie expresses concern about Vickey and Alice going home, Maggie says there is no real worry as Hobson will be making straight for The Moonraker's and will remember little of what he has said when he returns.

The two couples prepare to leave, despite Will's reluctance to let them go. Maggie repeats the promise to come to their weddings, but shows she knows her sisters well. There will be little contact afterwards, despite their gratitude to her now, as her sisters will be *too grand* for her and Will. She also hints at her ambitions for her future with Will, saying that they will be busy at work and predicting that it won't be long before they catch up with the other grand young couples.

❍ Compare Hobson's predictions for the future with Maggie's. Which do you think are more likely to come true? Keep these in mind when you read Act 4 and see if you were correct!

WILL'S EDUCATION CONTINUES (PP. 57–9)

Maggie repeats to Will that one day he will more successful than either of his brothers-in-law. That this is their wedding night will not hinder his progress. Will is learning to write as schoolchildren did in Victorian times, by copying sentences on to a slate. The sentences Maggie has chosen are intended to fill him with self-belief and ambition at the same time as teaching him his letters. The night before, he was writing *There is always room at the top*. Tonight's sentence is similarly encouraging: *Great things grow from small*. This is as much about the growth of his love for her as the future success of the business.

Maggie reveals a softer, romantic side to her character. She is about to throw out the flowers to clear the table for work, an act that reminds us of her criticism of the fancy buckle on the slipper, but she keeps one flower *to press in my Bible for a keepsake*. It is not only Will who changes because of their life together. Maggie seems to have discovered romance, if not in courtship, then in marriage. She continues in a similar way as she yawns and says the washing-up will wait till the morning, then tells Will to finish his writing while she gets ready for bed.

He is too shy to know what to do next. He begins to undress in the living room, looking all the time at the bedroom door. He cannot decide how to open it and walk in. He lies down to sleep on the sofa. Once again, Maggie takes the lead in an area of experience which is assumed to be the man's role. She comes out of the bedroom with her hair down, in her nightgown, emphasizing her femininity. Then, in a very unfeminine way, she takes Will *by the ear* and leads him into the bedroom. The humour of this, and the extent to which it acts as a symbol of the married relationship of this couple, makes this moment very effective in performance.

Test yourself

? How much does Albert ask Hobson to pay to settle his case? How much does Maggie say he should pay?

? Why is Hobson furious when he leaves and what does he threaten to do?

? Is Maggie a bully, or is there more to her than this? What reasons does she have for seeking to control all the men in her life?

? What changes in Will's character can you add to your Mind Map after reading Act 3?

Now enjoy the second interval before finding out just how low Hobson can sink.

Act 4, Success (pp. 60–82)

◆ Stage setting: Hobson's living room.
◆ The continuing fall of Henry Hobson and his business.
◆ Doctor MacFarlane diagnoses Hobson's alcoholism; prescribes Maggie as a cure.
◆ The sisters discuss who should come back to Hobson.
◆ The change in Will surprises Vickey and Alice.
◆ Will agrees terms with Hobson.
◆ Will and Maggie: an equal marriage.

THE STAGE SET (P. 60)

Place: This is the third, and final, set: Hobson's living room behind the shop. It contrasts with the simple accommodation of Maggie and Will. There is a stuffed armchair and matching cushioned seats, compared with the cast-offs Will mended. Cloths – anti-macassars – protect the chairs from the men's macassar hair oil. There are three portraits: Queen Victoria, her husband Prince Albert, and Lord Beaconsfield (also known as Disraeli, a Tory prime minister).

The room lacks female taste, as Hobson has kept to his threat of running his shop with men only as staff; it is also untidy and dirty, unlike Maggie's cellar.

Time: It is eight in the morning, and the lighting will indicate this.

The characters: Passing time has seen changes in Hobson's circumstances. Tubby Wadlow is setting the table for breakfast, and frying bacon – doing neither very well. Cooking over the fire, rather than in the kitchen, further indicates an all-male household. ❂ Sketch the stage set to emphasize the squalor of the situation.

THE CONTINUING FALL OF HENRY HOBSON (PP. 60–3)

The scene echoes the opening of Act 1 when Hobson needed *reviving* after a night's drinking. Again he has a hangover, hence Tubby's comment about his being *short-tempered*. Earlier, Hobson felt ill enough to summon the doctor and Jim Heeler to his bedside, but by the time Jim arrives, Hobson is on his way down for breakfast. Tubby complains that neither the business nor Mr Hobson are as they used to be.

Tubby and Jim discuss the reasons for the demise of Hobson's. Tubby blames Hobson's *temper and obstinacy*. He denies that Mossop's rival business is the main cause. A major problem is that now there are only men in the shop, losing the remaining high-class trade: men prefer to be served by a woman, and *ladies that are ladies* prefer the help of their own sex to try on shoes – someone like Maggie. ❂ Does Tubby's argument seem reasonable?

The conversation is interrupted by Hobson – as unkempt as his surroundings. Jim comments that a man in this state needs a woman's care. Tubby suggests going for Maggie.

The depths to which Hobson has sunk are evident when, confronted by the bacon, he agrees because he is *a dying man*. He exaggerates his illness, describing how he has been unable to wash or shave, as both made him think of suicide. He identifies the cause of his depression in one word: *Moonraker's*. Jim is defensive, because his habits are identical to Hobson's: a *regular* drinker, though not, he hopes, a *toper* who drinks to excess. It could be him next. ❂ What do you already know about the consequences of Hobson's drinking which show it is excessive?

HOBSON'S ALCOHOLISM IS DIAGNOSED (PP. 64–7)

Tubby returns alongside Doctor MacFarlane, a character whose main purpose is to confirm the cause of Hobson's sickness. He bluntly expresses annoyance at finding his patient well enough to be out of bed, having been up all night delivering a baby. He initially thinks Jim is his patient, then, realizing his mistake, remarks that Hobson and Heeler do not have *much to choose between* them: their looks confirm their heavy drinking.

Hobson meets his match in a character as stubborn as himself. He ought to have seen a doctor before and he is *a fool* not to have realized this; his complaint and his character *are the same*, his personality is the cause of his drinking. Doctor MacFarlane then makes to leave, despite Jim's protests.

Hobson answers the doctor's questions evasively, though revealing that he is depressed – even suicidal. The doctor is pushed into stating his diagnosis: *chronic alcoholism ... a serious case*. Hobson accepts the truth of this, but is less receptive to any of the three elements of the cure Doctor MacFarlane prescribes: medicine, tee-totalism (giving up alcohol completely), and – in the absence of a wife – Maggie to make him stick to his cure. It is ironic that Hobson objects to the medicine because he is *particular* about what he puts into his stomach. ❂ How does this scene remind you of the meaning of the phrase 'Hobson's choice' (see p. 24.)? What realistic choices does Hobson have?

Right on cue, Maggie arrives. The doctor needs one look to sum up her suitability for the cure. He reminds us that Maggie will be sacrificing the independence of her marital home, which Hobson dismisses as only *two cellars in Oldfield Road*. She will also be doing her father a kindness he has hardly earned, but the fact is, she has a choice, while her father, if he is to live, now has no choice at all. ❂ Do you think Maggie ought to come back? Why?

THE SISTERS DISCUSS WHO SHOULD COME BACK TO HOBSON (PP. 70–4)

Hobson says he cannot give up alcohol because it is his custom and because of his age, neither of these being logical explanations. Maggie tells him she can make him give up, but she has to consult Will about returning. Hobson can hardly believe that Maggie will take Will's views into account.

Hobson attempts to be the man of the house: telling her it is her duty to return because she is the eldest and that his claims as a father are more important than those of a husband. Alice's arrival reminds us that Maggie is not Hobson's only daughter. Marriage to a *fashionable solicitor* has made Alice even more snobbish. She is dressed to impress and is described as *languidly haughty*.

She dismisses her father's ill health, saying that he has *quite a colour* (a flushed face is symptom of drinking: she has little idea of what is wrong with him). When Maggie tells her one of the sisters must return, Alice's excuse is instant, selfish, and reflects her proud appearance.

Vickey greets her father with a show of affection. Hobson is delighted that at least his youngest child cares for him, but as soon as he mentions that she might return, the hugs stop. Her reasons are more personal than Alice's and are whispered to Maggie. In the coy manner of Victorian times, pregnancy is not discussed in the presence of a man, so Maggie sends her father out of the room.

Maggie sums up the selfishness of her sisters. They repeat Hobson's reasons: Alice says it is Maggie's duty and Vickey points out that Maggie's cellar home is less to lose than theirs. Maggie reiterates that it is not her decision but her husband's and Vickey is ruder than Hobson saying, 'Will Mossop hasn't the spirit of a louse.' Maggie reminds her and the audience that Will has *maybe come on*. This is her cue to leave the room as she hears Will enter the shop.

The younger sisters are even more selfish when they talk together. Neither of them seems concerned about their father. Vickey's main worry is that Maggie and Will could inherit a bigger portion of his legacy if he dies. Alice is on the same greedy wavelength and says that Albert should draw up a will immediately. Maggie's chief concern is that her father should live, so it is unlikely that death and inheritance have even crossed her mind.

What can you remember?

? What evidence can you find from pp. 60–3 that Hobson and his business are in serious difficulties?

? What are the three elements of Doctor MacFarlane's treatment for Hobson's illness? Which one is most important?

? How do Maggie's reasons compare with the reasons her sisters give not to return? Which of the three sisters (if any) do you think ought to come back and why?

Take a short break before you find out how a year of Maggie's influence has changed Will.

THE CHANGE IN WILL SURPRISES VICKEY AND ALICE (PP. 74–6)

Will has literally gone up in the world when Vickey first sees him: he is up a ladder examining Hobson's stock, and his answer to her question rings from off-stage with a new confidence and decisiveness. He is assessing what he is *coming into* before deciding whether he and Maggie should return. Alice is astonished; Vickey is defensive: she has not realized that Will and Maggie would expect to return to the business as well as to Hobson's home.

Will's appearance on stage is all his words promised. The stage direction says he is *prosperous* and his progress is immediately evident. He now leads and Maggie follows. (He does forget to remove his hat, but she quietly puts that right!) He instructs her to bring her father and to *be sharp* about it, as he is busier in his shop than Hobson is. Will now socializes with other shopkeepers and knows what they say about Hobson's. He values the business at *about two hundred* pounds, and he knows just how much the business has deteriorated.

The social difference that separates Will and his sisters-in-law is indicated: Alice is ignorant of these facts because she has *married into the law* though he would expect Vickey to be more aware, being married to a shopkeeper. Vickey's snobbish remark that wholesale grocery is *business, not trade* shows how defensive Will's confidence makes her feel. ✪ What does this conversation show us about how Will has changed?

Maggie's proposed return stands to benefit Will: he is in a good bargaining position as Hobson needs Maggie far more than Will needs Hobson's. The younger sisters are furious, especially Alice. She pulls rank, retorting that she has the status of being married to a successful solicitor, '*I'm Mrs Albert Prosser*.' Will is quick to reply that he is now known by many as Mr Mossop, echoing Maggie's comment that her sisters are *privileged* to call him by his first name.

WILL AGREES TERMS WITH HOBSON (PP. 76–81)

The sisters are reduced to sulky defeat when Hobson arrives and it does not take Will long to infuriate him, too. Will has stood up to Hobson before, but the confidence with which he orders him about now is still a surprise. His lack of sympathy for Hobson even provokes Maggie to exclaim in shock, causing Will almost to undermine his position by revealing that he is following Maggie's instructions to *take a high hand*.

Hobson responds with temper to his decisive, plain-speaking son-in-law. He suggests his younger daughters should leave. He is so confident that he can get his way with Will that he asks Alice and Vickey outright if they will return, suggesting that dutiful, loving daughters ought to have jumped at the opportunity – or even *skipped like a calf by the cedars of Lebanon*, a phrase from the Bible, humorously exaggerated in such circumstances.

Both sisters answer with an unadorned No. Hobson tells them to go and Will shows them out. They are furious, so when Maggie annoys Vickey by suggesting they may lower themselves sufficiently to come to tea sometime, Vickey's parting comment is the insult *Beggars on horseback*. This implies that Maggie and Will are behaving in a manner above their station, which is ironic: if anyone can be described as having *stiff necks with pride*, it is Vickey and Alice. ✪ Does Hobson's display of male authority convince you?

Now he feels in control, Hobson offers to take Will and Maggie back on pretty much the terms they left: they can have the back bedroom; Maggie can do the housekeeping; Will can have his old job back for the old pay, and the two men will split the housekeeping costs between them. Hobson describes this offer as generous. ✪ Is it? How is Will likely to react?

Will's response is instantaneous: he stands and gives the simple command, 'Come home, Maggie.' Hobson is amazed. Will spells out their success in his longest speech; compare it with his wedding speech and you can see his personal progress too. In just one year he and Maggie have made enough profit to pay back Mrs Hepworth's loan and to make *a bit o' brass* too. He has taken Hobson's high-class trade away, despite his shop's location. It would take more incentive than his old job to give up the business that has destroyed Hobson's. Hobson struggles to grasp the change in his *old shoe-hand*.

Will proposes his terms decisively. He repeats Hobson's word *generous* and offers him a partnership provided he does not interfere (a *sleeping partner*). This is more like a deal than what Hobson offered: a share in a thriving enterprise, merely for providing the premises. He concludes that the shop will be renamed *William Mossop, late Hobson*.

Hobson is still struggling to come to terms with Will's suggestions, but the discussion between Will and Maggie assumes that only the name now needs to be decided. Maggie suggests *Hobson and Mossop*, trying to offer her father some last shreds of respect. Will is masterful. He will compromise only as far as *Mossop and Hobson*, or he and Maggie return to Oldfield Road. Maggie agrees; Hobson only has time to splutter '*But ...*' before Will moves on, describing improvements to the shop. When Hobson asks him sarcastically if he thinks he is in St Ann's Square, Will's reply shows his ambition. It seems quite likely that he will become the richest of the three young men. As if he does a business takeover every day, Will breezily suggests that Maggie and Hobson go to have the partnership deed drawn up. ✪ Would Will have been capable of any of this if he had married Ada?

Hobson is defeated. The title of the play assumes its full significance here, for Hobson knows he has no choice but to agree to everything. He is described as looking *pathetically* at the two of them, then *obediently* going to find his hat. Will's genuine kindness is shown as he confesses that he fears he has crushed Hobson.

AN EQUAL MARRIAGE (PP. 81–2)

Will's frankness is touching. He admits this was an act though, to his surprise, he sounded as if he meant what he said. '*Didn't you?*' asks Maggie, making him reflect that, in fact, he probably did! He used the power he gained through Maggie, but there is no doubt that this power is now his own: he will soon accept the *outrageous big idea* that he is the new *Master of Hobson's*.

He seeks Maggie's reassurance, admitting that he quite scared himself, particularly when it came to arguing with her! She affectionately stops him, telling him how proud she is of him.

He responds by emphasizing his pride in her and says that one improvement he wishes to make is to replace her brass wedding ring with a gold one. The romance in Maggie shows when she says she will wear the new one only *for show*: the brass one is never to leave her finger. It will be a life-long reminder of how they started out. Their exchange of affectionate words and a kiss leaves us in no doubt of their love for each other. Maggie was quite right: the romance of courting is not necessary before a very happy marriage. For this couple, romance has grown steadily after the event.

Hobson and Maggie leave for Albert Prosser's and Will repeats the words with which he responded to Maggie's proposal, but here his *amazement, triumph and incredulity* are *not in the same street* as his feelings then as he exclaims, '*By gum!*'

Think about your final impression

? Design costumes for the following characters to wear in Act 4: Will, Hobson, Vickey, Alice, Maggie. Compare these with their costumes in Act 1. Note down how their dress reflects their developing character traits.

? What was the deal Hobson offered to Will if he returned? What did Will offer to Hobson? Why was Hobson's offer mean and Will's generous?

? How well can you remember the whole play? Note down in the boxes opposite why each of these places is important. Who lives there? What happened there?

Reward yourself for working through the whole Commentary — you deserve a break!

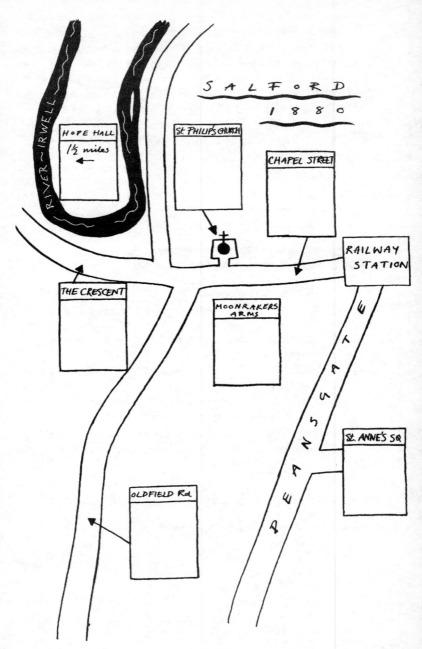

SALFORD
1880

HOPE HALL
1½ miles

RIVER ~ IRWELL

St PHILIPS CHURCH

CHAPEL STREET

RAILWAY STATION

THE CRESCENT

MOONRAKERS ARMS

DEANSGATE

St. ANNE'S SQ

OLDFIELD Rd

74

TOPICS FOR DISCUSSION AND BRAINSTORMING

One of the best ways to revise is with one or more friends. Even if you're with someone who hardly knows the text, having to explain things to your friend will help you to organize your own thoughts and memorize key points. If you're with someone who knows the text, you'll be able to help each other.

Discussion will also help you to develop interesting new ideas that perhaps neither of you would have had alone. Use a brainstorming approach to tackle any of the topics listed below. Allow yourself to share whatever ideas come into your head – however silly they seem. This will get you thinking creatively.

Whether alone or with a friend, use Mind Mapping (see p. vi) to help you brainstorm and organize your ideas. If with a friend, use a large sheet of paper and coloured pens.

Any of the topics here could be set for coursework or feature in an exam paper, but even if you think you've found a similar question, do make sure you plan your answer for the precise question given.

TOPICS

1 Suppose Maggie kept a diary, write three days' entries giving a detailed description of the events and her feelings about them for: the day she proposed to Will, her Wedding Day, the day Will took over Hobson's.
2 Describe how Will Mossop changes from the tongue-tied, timid workman of Act 1 to the prosperous confident businessman of Act 4. (See pp. 47 and 51 for ideas for a Mind Map about Will.)
3 Comment on the exploration of different ideas about love and marriage in *Hobson's Choice*.
4 Explain the meaning of the title of *Hobson's Choice* and comment upon the way Brighouse develops this as a theme of the play.
5 Discuss the use of regional forms of language in the play, and explain what it contributes to a performance of the play on stage.

In all your study, in coursework, and in exams, be aware of the following:

- **Characterization** – the characters and how we know about them (e.g. what they say and do, how the author describes them), their relationships, and how they develop.
- **Plot and structure** – what happens and how it is organized into parts or episodes.
- **Setting and atmosphere** – the changing scene and how it reflects the story (e.g. a rugged landscape and storm reflecting a character's emotional difficulties).
- **Style and language** – the author's choice of words, and literary devices such as imagery, and how these reflect the mood.
- **Viewpoint** – how the story is told (e.g. through an imaginary narrator, or in the third person but through the eyes of one character – 'She was furious – how dare he!').
- **Social and historical context** – influences on the author (see 'Background' in this guide).

Develop your ability to:

- Relate **detail** to **broader content, meaning and style**.
- Show understanding of the author's **intentions, technique and meaning** (brief and appropriate comparisons with other works by the same author will gain marks).
- Give **personal response and interpretation**, backed up by **examples** and short **quotations**.
- **Evaluate** the author's achievement (how far does the author succeed and why?)

Make sure you:

- Know how to use paragraphs correctly.
- Use a wide range of vocabulary and sentence structure.
- Use **short** appropriate quotations as evidence of your understanding of that part of the text.
- Use literary terms to show your understanding of what the author is trying to achieve with language.

THE EXAM ESSAY

Planning

You will probably have about an hour for one essay. It is worth spending about ten minutes planning it. An excellent way to do this is in the three stages below.

1 **Mind Map** your ideas, without worrying about their order yet.
2 **Order** the relevant ideas (the ones that really relate to the question) by numbering them in the order in which you will write the essay.
3 **Gather** your evidence and short quotes.

You could remember this as the **MOG** technique.

Then write the essay, allowing five minutes at the end for checking relevance, and spelling, grammar and punctuation.

REMEMBER!

Stick to the question, and always **back up** your points with evidence in the form of examples and short quotations. Note: you can use '. . .' for unimportant words missed out in a quotation.

Model answer and plan

The next (and final) chapter consists of a model answer to an exam question on *Hobson's Choice*, together with the Mind Map and essay plan used to write it. Don't be put off if you don't think you could write an essay to this standard yet. You'll develop your skills if you work at them. Even if you're reading this the night before the exam, you can easily memorize the MOG technique in order to do your personal best.

The model answer and essay plan are good examples for you to follow, but don't try to learn them off by heart. It's better to pay close attention to the wording of the question you choose to answer in the exam, and allow Mind Mapping to help you to think creatively.

Before reading the answer, you might like to do a plan of your own, then compare it with the example. The numbered points, with comments at the end, show why it's a good answer.

QUESTION

How do Henry Hobson and Will Mossop behave towards each other in Act 1? How do their attitudes change as the play progresses?

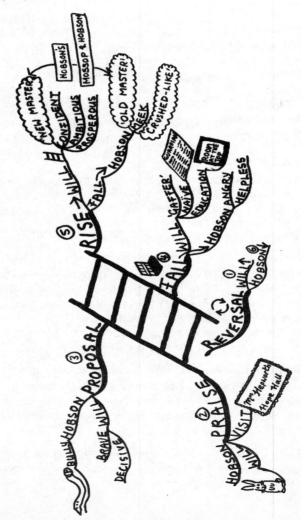

PLAN

1 Will and Hobson – reversal of roles – power struggle.
2 Mrs Hepworth's visit – Hobson in charge – Will meek.
3 Changes after Maggie's proposal – Hobson aggressive – Will stands up to him.
4 After Hobson's fall – Hobson needs help – Will plays role of 'gaffer'.
5 Will becomes 'master' of Hobson's – Hobson is defeated.
6 Compare Act 1 with Act 4 – reversal of 2 – similarities with 3.

ESSAY

The relationship between Will Mossop and Henry Hobson is intriguing as it undergoes a complete reversal of roles during the year of the play's action. Initially Hobson is Will's boss, the owner of a successful shoe shop, while Will is a mere bootmaker in Hobson's cellar workshop; but by the end, Will has taken over Hobson's business and Hobson is left powerless.[1]

The two characters first appear together when Mrs Hepworth enquires about who made the boots she is wearing. Hobson assumes that she has come to complain and, upon discovering that Will made the boots, he tells her he is capable of 'making the man suffer for it'. Hobson is a domineering character who likes to feel in control of his family and business.[2] Will must be used to Hobson's temper. He seems terrified as he pops up out of the cellar trap-door, and ducks as if expecting a blow when Mrs Hepworth offers her visiting card.

When Mrs Hepworth praises Will's workmanship, Hobson's attitude changes: he answers for Will, promising that he is always to make Mrs Hepworth's boots in future and that he 'won't make a change' by moving elsewhere to work (comments which prove to be ironic as the play progresses).[3] When she suggests that Will is underpaid, Hobson sends him away and, as soon as she has left, angrily complains that praise makes workmen 'uppish'. He prefers his men (like he prefers his daughters) servile.[4] Will has no chance of compliments or a pay rise in recognition of his talents from Hobson.

Their next encounter later the same day is in circumstances neither would have predicted: Maggie has more or less forced

Will to agree to marry her. Hobson is incensed at the idea of this 'come-by-chance' (meaning that Will's father has the stigma of being born illegitimate in a Victorian institution[5]) being a member of his family. He says it will make him a laughing stock in the area. Unable to beat his daughter because she is 'female and exempt', he threatens to beat Will every morning until he forgets all ideas of marriage to Maggie. Will's behaviour is the opposite of what we expect from the timid man who Mrs Hepworth described as 'like a rabbit'.[6] He does not back down and retreat to the cellar; instead he argues with Hobson. When Hobson threatens him with the belt he stands his ground, promising to 'take her quick ... and stick to her like glue' if Hobson strikes him. Furious, Hobson lashes out. Will responds with equal fire, kissing Maggie. He threatens that if Hobson strikes him again, the couple will walk out and set up in business together. Both men seem amazed by this unexpected turn of events, though Maggie is delighted, telling Will she knew he had this potential.[4]

Both men must carry out their threats, for, a month later, Maggie and Will have a business and home of their own. When Hobson and Will next meet, it is in these changed circumstances. On Maggie and Will's wedding day, Hobson seeks her help with the legal problems resulting from his fall into Beenstock's storeroom.[4] Maggie reminds Will that he is 'gaffer here' and he plays the part confidently, inviting Hobson in and offering him tea and pork pie.[2] Will takes an intelligent interest and makes Hobson realise how embarrassing the consequences could be when he speculates about the publicity the newspapers might give to the court case. Hobson almost loses his temper with Will, but calms down when Maggie reminds him he needs help. He cannot afford to lose their co-operation again with his bad temper.[7] As he leaves, having discovered the trick his three daughters and Alice's lawyer husband-to-be have played on him, his attitude to Will is interesting: 'I'm sorry for you ...You're the best of the bunch ... you know your trade and it's an honest one.' The connection between the two men hints the outcome of the play to the audience.[8]

Their next meeting soon shows that Hobson's assessment of Will as 'a backward lad' was inaccurate. A year later Hobson has nearly killed himself with drink and his business has all but been destroyed by competition from Will's. The two men again meet because Hobson needs help: the doctor has told him one of his daughters must return to care for him and the younger two have made it clear that they will not.[4] Maggie, again, puts Will in the position of 'gaffer' saying it is his decision, not hers. The costumes of Will and Hobson are a sharp contrast, a reversal of how they were dressed in Act 1: Hobson appears 'unshaven and collarless' whilst Will now looks 'prosperous' with his hat and air of self-confidence.[9] Will speaks to Hobson with confidence, too: 'I'm worried about your life ... but I'm none worried that bad I'll see my business suffer.[2]

Hobson states, wrongly, he has 'fight enough ... for a dozen such as him'. When he offers to take Maggie and Will back on the same terms as they left, Will as an 'eighteen shilling a week bootmaker',[6, 7] Will reacts decisively. He knows that his business has reduced Hobson's to a total value of only about two hundred pounds.[4] Hobson is in no position to negotiate anything, as Will has everything Hobson lacks. His offer to move his business to Hobson's address and make him a sleeping partner is very generous, though Hobson is unable to adjust to such a changed relationship: 'But – but – you're Will Mossop ... my old shoe hand.' Even the name of the shop is discussed with Maggie, as Hobson blusters and protests, to no avail. By the time the legal arrangements are mentioned, Hobson knows he is defeated. Will's attitude then is more sympathetic than gloating: 'He's crushed-like ... I bore on him too hard.'[6]

The end of Act 4 reflects the end of Act 1 in several ways: Maggie's pride in Will, Will's amazement at his own achievement and Hobson's surprise at the unexpected outcome of events. However, it is a complete reversal of their first encounter, for Will is now the new 'master of Hobson's', whilst Henry Hobson is the meek, obedient one of the pair.[10]

WHAT'S SO GOOD ABOUT IT?

1 Introduction shows a firm grasp of the meaning of the question.
2 Understanding of character.

3 Awareness of literary terms.
4 Shows thorough knowledge of the text.
5 Relevant historical background knowledge.
6 Good use of relevant quotation.
7 Refers back to an earlier incident.
8 Awareness of audience response.
9 Perceptive comment relevant to play as performance.
10 Good conclusion – shows firm grasp of structure.

GLOSSARY OF LITERARY TERMS

accent   the way someone pronounces words, influenced by background.

alliteration   repetition of a sound at the beginnings of words, e.g. *low over the land*.

comedy of manners   a type of drama exploring everyday life and behaviour, sometimes through humourous exaggeration.

context   the social and historical influences on the author.

dialect   a regional form of speech including vocabulary and grammar differing from standard English.

dramatic irony   where the audience knows something not known by one or more of the characters.

foreshadowing   an indirect warning of things to come, often through imagery.

image   a word picture used to make an idea come alive; e.g. a **metaphor**, **simile**, or **personification** (see separate entries).

imagery   the kind of word picture used to make an idea come alive.

ironic reversal   when a character's traits are emphasized (often humorously) by their changing to the reverse of their normal form; e.g. Hobson fawning on Mrs Hepworth.

irony   (1) where the author or a character says the opposite of what they really think, or pretends ignorance of the true facts, usually for the sake of humour or ridicule; (2) where events turn out in what seems a particularly inappropriate way, as if mocking human effort. (See also **dramatic irony**.)

metaphor   a description of a thing as if it were something essentially different but also in some way similar; e.g. Hobson tells the doctor: *So now you can go, with your tail between your legs* (like a scolded dog).

monosyllables   words with only one syllable; e.g. *make white show as black.*

personification   a description of a thing as if it were a person; e.g. *the sun was hiding.*

prose   language in which, unlike verse, there is no set number of syllables in a line, and no rhyming.

setting   the place in which the action occurs, usually affecting the atmosphere; e.g. the shop.

simile   a comparison of two things different in most ways but somehow similar; e.g. Mrs Hepworth says of Will, *He's like a rabbit.*

structure   the overall pattern of the plot.

symbol   an object used by a writer to represent something abstract; e.g. the ladder on which Will stands, showing how he is going up in the world.

theme   an idea explored by an author; e.g. love and marriage.

viewpoint   how the story is told; e.g. through action, or in discussion between characters.

NDEX

Page references in bold denote major character or theme sections.

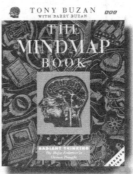